THE DAY'S BURDEN
STUDIES, LITERARY & POLITICAL
AND MISCELLANEOUS ESSAYS

THE DAY'S BURDEN
STUDIES, LITERARY & POLITICAL
AND MISCELLANEOUS ESSAYS
BY THOMAS M. KETTLE

Second Edition

PR
6021
.E75
D3
1968

Essay Index Reprint Series

97281

BOOKS FOR LIBRARIES PRESS
FREEPORT, NEW YORK

Second Edition

First Published 1918
Reprinted 1968

LIBRARY OF CONGRESS CATALOG CARD NUMBER:
68-54353

PRINTED IN THE UNITED STATES OF AMERICA

CONTENTS

THE DAY'S BURDEN

MISCELLANEOUS ESSAYS

THE DAY'S BURDEN: STUDIES LITERARY AND POLITICAL, appeared in 1910, when the late Lieutenant Kettle was a brilliant young member of the Nationalist Parliamentary Party. The book has been for a considerable time out of print; and its contents are now, with the exception of a few pages on "Reason in Rhyme," republished in this volume of collected essays, together with a number of studies contributed to the Press between 1910 and the outbreak of the war. In 1912 "A Man Troubled About Everything" (*Public Opinion*), and "The Day of All the Dead" (*Freeman's Journal*); in 1913 "The Economics of Nationalism" (*Irish Ecclesiastical Record*), "The Importance of Being Narrow-minded" (*Public Opinion*); in 1914 "The World of the Blind" and "The Unimportance of Politics" (*British Review*), "Labour and Civilization," and "Labour: War or Peace?" recall the labour troubles of 1913-14, and particularly the great Dublin strike, in which Mr. Kettle took so vigourous an interest. Both appeared in *The Dublin Review*—1918.

THE DAY'S BURDEN

TO MY WIFE

" *Not the sea, only wrecks the hopes of men,*
Look deeper, there is shipwreck everywhere " :
So mourned the exquisite Roman's rich despair,
Too high in death for that ignoble pen.
Nero, his wrecker, is amply wrecked since then,
And all that Rome's a whiff of charnel air;
But to subdue Petronius' mal-de-mer
Have we found drugs? I pray you, What? and When?
Shipwreck, one grieves to say, retains its vogue :
Or let the keel win on in stouter fashion,
And look! your golden lie of Tir-na-n'Og
Is sunset and waste waters, chill and ashen—
Faith lasts? Nay, since I knew your yielded eyes,
I am content with sight .... of Paradise.

APOLOGY

The papers collected here have, for the most part, already appeared in various journals and reviews. I am indebted to the courtesy of the *Morning Leader*, the *New Ireland Review*, the *Fortnightly Review*, and Messrs. Maunsel & Co., for leave to re-publish them. In all cases there has been a good deal of revision and re-writing, and an attempt has been made to impress a certain unity on the constituent materials such as may reasonably be looked for in anything that calls itself a book. The study of Otto Effertz appears for the first time, and is, indeed, as far as I know, the only account that has yet been given in English of that bizarre but brilliant pioneer. Topical articles on Egyptian Nationalism and International Socialism have been included because they give a glimpse of movements which, so far as one can judge, are certain to endure, and of leaders whose influence is likely to grow rather than to diminish in the immediate future.

For title I have ventured to use THE DAY'S BURDEN because that seems to me to be the most characteristic thing about the day, and because all these essays are concerned with "problems"—economic, political, and literary. To anyone who, glancing at the foreign names which recur in these pages, asks with a sniff of contempt, "What has all this got to do with Ireland?" I do not know what reply to make. Something like this, perhaps: Ireland, a small nation, is, none the less, large enough to contain all the complexities of the twentieth century. There is no ecstasy and no agony of the modern soul remote from her experience; there is none of all the difficulties which beset men, eager to build at last a wise and stable society, that she has not encountered. In some of them she has even been the forerunner of the world. If this generation has, for its first task, the recovery of the old Ireland, it has, for its second, the discovery of the new Europe. Ireland awaits her Goethe—but in Ireland he must not be a Pagan —who will one day arise to teach her that while a strong people has its own self for centre, it has the universe for circumference. All cultures belong to a nation that has once taken sure hold of its own culture. A national literature that seeks to found itself in isolation from the general life of humanity can only produce the pale and waxen growths of a plant isolated from the sunlight. In gaining her own soul Ireland will gain the whole world. Till that Goethe is born, and the new fabric begins to rise under his inspiration, we must go on shovelling together our trivial heaps of sand and rubble.

That is all I would dare to say in placation of the contemptuous sniff. Originality is a toy that no goddess left in my cradle. My only programme for Ireland consists, in equal parts, of Home Rule and the Ten Commandments. My only counsel to Ireland is, that in order to become deeply Irish, she must become European.

October 1910.

THE PHILOSOPHY OF POLITICS [1]

The subject I have chosen for my paper is almost an insult to your intelligence. I could occupy the whole time at my disposal by merely reading you a list of writers who have devoted themselves to the establishment of a science of politics, and among them you would find, from Aristotle downwards, the masters and shapers of human thought. What then must you think of the audacity of an attempt, with the inadequate time and the infinitely inadequate resources at my command, to give some account not merely of political science but of the philosophical ideas on which it rests? I know, however, that I can count on your indulgence. And I would ask you to accept the title of this paper in a large and charitable way, and to forgive its pretentiousness.

It does seem to me that a political society like this is under the obligation of taking an occasional bath in the sea of fundamental ideas. Practical people regard such a proceeding, it must be admitted, with extreme distrust. If one desires an early and extensive unpopularity there is no surer way to it than to insist on analyzing received principles. Our mothers, you will remember, used to have the strangest objection to our taking their watches to pieces. They rather doubted our competence to put the springs and wheels together again. Society experiences much the same state of mind with regard

[1] Presidential Address before the Young Ireland Branch of the United Irish League, December 1905.

B

to the attempt to reduce it to terms of mere reason. Society is right, but it is only the nineteenth century that has made its attitude possible. It needed a long development of psychological and historical study to make us understand that reason is but one faculty of a many-facultied being; that the forces which used to be brusquely dismissed as mere sentiment, mere instinct, mere enthusiasm, are inseparable elements of human nature. We have come to realize, in a word, that life is incomparably vaster, more various, and more complex than any theory of it. I dwell on this because it has a special bearing on our subject. In approaching political science we must remember that it does not profess to reproduce the rich detail of life in society, but stands to it rather as a chart to an ocean or a mathematical formula to the path of a planet. Still, if reason has abandoned the tyranny which it once aimed at, its call can none the less be denied. We must render ourselves some rational account of the forces by which and among which we live. Among the greatest of these is the society, the political framework, in which we are born and in which our lives are cast. Call yourself a non-politician as loudly as you choose, you will never succeed in ignoring politics; therefore of necessity an attempt must be made to understand them. What is the object of politics, what we are justified in expecting it to do and what it cannot do, what part it should play in the life of the individual modern man, and what is the temper in which a wise man will approach it—these are questions neither remote nor abstract, but questions that come knocking at your door and mine, and that have to be answered. All I can hope to do to-night is to suggest, in a random and completely undogmatic fashion, points of view from which politics may be regarded, and principles by which the efficiency of institutions may be tested.

PHILOSOPHY OF POLITICS

When we speak of politics as a science we must remember that the word is used with a difference. The characteristic note of a natural science is its ability to predict with mathematical accuracy. Such prophetic power cannot be attributed to politics. The stupendous complexity of the subject-matter, the endless chain of action and interaction make it impossible to gather all the data necessary for certainty. And then that unpredictable element called free-will is constantly interloping to upset the logic of your determinist drama. Still there are large principles which seem to approach the certainty of physical laws. One can find a ready illustration in what we very properly heard a great deal about at the Convention the other day, the need for unity. That without unity—of action, of course, for absolute unity of thought and feeling we neither can have, nor should demand—a political party must be ineffective is surely just as certain as any law of chemistry or physics? The principle it embodies is one implicit in the constitution of every state, namely, that the will of the majority of duly chosen representatives must, as regards action, prevail over the will of the minority. Deny that principle and you cannot pass a single legislative Act ; you cannot levy a single tax. In the long history of English insolence there is hardly anything else so insolent as Mr. Balfour's demand with regard to our University Question. He said, you will remember, that no Bill could be introduced to realize this reform unless there was absolute unanimity among all interested parties in Ireland. Had he applied that maxim consistently to English political life, to political life anywhere, the result would be that no government could continue for twelve hours. In proclaiming it Mr. Balfour was proclaiming himself an Anarchist. This principle, then, that the will of the majority, registered in the due forms and under the due safe-

3

guards of individual freedom, must prevail over the
will of the minority affords a good example of the
sort of established law we can hope for in political
science.

I pass on to the fundamental question : What is
the object of politics ? Politics in its largest sense
includes the whole control and management of
public affairs by the government in power, together
with the whoie process of agitation by which the
masses of people not in power seek to influence
and alter the conduct of things. Now, if you look
in the text-books you will find that the object of
government is order. But what is the object of
order ? That is a point which ought to be considered by the inflamed gentlemen from the West
of Ireland who write letters signed "A Disgusted
Loyalist" to the *Irish Times* demanding the vindi-
cation of what they call "law and order." Law
and order are not absolutes, but merely means to
an end. To mistake them for ends in themselves
is to regard the shell as the important element in
the egg, the fence as the important element in the
field. The cry of "Order for Order's sake" is as
ruinously foolish as that of art for art's sake, or
money for money's sake. It is for the sake of
humanity that all these must exist. Behind order
there is life, and it is only in so far as it tends to
increase the sum and improve the quality of life
that any system of government or scheme of positive
law is ethically justifiable. If you analyse the rights
commonly regarded as essential and inalienable—
the right to property, to personal safety, to marriage
—you will find as the common source of them all
this right to life. And by life I mean not merely
physical existence, but that rich human existence
which can be had only in community, that sort of
life which Edmund Burke had in mind when he
described the State as "a partnership in all science,

4

a partnership in all art, a partnership in every
virtue, and in all perfection."

You will say, perhaps, that this test of government—*Does it forward life?*—is vague. Life, even
in the biological sense, has not been defined. That
is perfectly true. But we do not demand, as I have
said, in politics the mapped-out mathematical
certainty of natural science. The average man
possesses a sufficiently clear notion for practical
purposes of the conditions that make life desirable,
beautiful, and worthy to be lived. A government
is good or bad, the order it maintains is the discipline of liberty or that of oppression, in so far as
it promotes or hinders the wide diffusion of these
conditions. I think you will find this test of *life* a
helpful one in your attempt to gather together in
some binding idea the currents of effort that make
up contemporary Ireland. Somebody has compared
the *rôle* of a general idea to that of a magnet. If
you bring a magnet into contact with a glass plate
on which there is a confused mass of iron filings it
immediately strains and sets them into regular
and beautiful patterns. The filings represent
the chaos of concrete facts that experience brings
thronging in on us, and the magnetic idea that
makes them intelligible, as it has created them, is
that of life. It is the one justificatory word on the
tongues of the emigrants as they stream down to the
ships. They "want to see life." By no mere accident is it that the Gaelic League which started with
language has gathered round it games, singing,
dancing, and all the arts of friendly intercourse.
These all stand for life, joyously realizing itself under
benign conditions. It has been said that all government exists to hang a fowl before the Sunday fire of
every peasant. Dancing is less necessary than eating,
and more beautiful. It represents the free energy
of a life that has not merely withstood but has

5

conquered the hostility of external circumstances, and you will understand the sense in which I say that all contemporary Irish movements exist in order to set a boy and a girl dancing at a Sunday *ceilidh*.

Analyze the agitation to break up the grass ranches and to give the land to the people and to the plough and you will find that it rests on two assumptions— not very daring assumptions! The first is that the life of a human being is more precious and worthier to be forwarded by the State than that of a bullock. The second is that if an individual persists in so using the property which society allows him to control, as to base his personal comfort and prosperity on the misery and degradation of others, while a cleaner way of living is open to him, then society has both the right and the duty to break his selfish monopoly.[1] For he has declared war on society, and has violated the obligations of the social bond.

This test of *life* changes our attitude towards positive law in general. Take the common description of life that it is a "continuous adjustment of internal

---

[1] *Cf.* Naudet, *Premiers Principes de Sociologie Catholique.* Bloud et Cie, Paris, 1904. P. 31. ''The Canon Law, as the great historian Janssen tells us, regarded property as a fief granted by God. This doctrine, founded on Scripture, involves the evident consequence that the owner of property is responsible before God for the use to which he puts his property. He must not use it after his mere caprice ; and the Popes as guardians of the law of justice have more than once asserted this principle against owners who had disregarded it. Thus we find Clement IV., in the thirteenth century, giving permission to any stranger to break up the third part of an estate which the owner persistently refused to till. Sixtus IV., in the fifteenth century, decrees that ' power is given in future and always to all and each to till and sow in the territory of Rome and the patrimony of St. Peter, in Tuscany as well as on the littoral of Campania, at the usual and proper times, one third of the uncultivated lands, to be chosen at will, whoever the landlord should be. . . .' It was held sufficient to have asked the landlord for leave to enter on the lands, even though this leave had been refused.'' Naudet cites Clement VII., Pius VI. and Pius VII. as having confirmed and renewed this insistence on the social duties of property.

6

to external relations" and apply it to human society, and, in its light, law loses its old iron absoluteness. It shows itself not as something fixed and immutable, but as an imperfect transcript of the moral conditions necessary to safeguard life, changing continually with these conditions. Ethical principles are, of course, invariable; but the formal enactments in which they are imperfectly embodied form a system, developing, as we hope, towards a fuller realization. It is the thought-climate, called in a large way evolution, and so characteristic of the nineteenth century, that has given us this new point of view. We have applied it to some pretensions of the law courts and seen them wither up; we might also extend it to some of the commonplaces of popular thought. There is not, I suppose, a more insistent and widespread demand with regard to Irish questions than that they should be "finally" settled. But once grasp the idea of a state as a living, developing organism, and this expectation of finality is seen to be a pure illusion. Popular thought is never altogether wrong, and of course there is an obvious sense in which, for example, a comprehensive measure of Home Rule might be regarded as a "final" settlement of our political status. Still, even in this case, the notion is illusory and misleading. Life is growth; growth is change; and the one thing of which we are certain is that society must keep moving on. Freedom is a battle and a march. It has many bivouacs, but no barracks. You remember the counsel given by the serving-man in the heroic tale to Diarmuid and Grainne. "In the place where you catch your food you must not cook it, and in the place where you cook it you must not eat it, and in the place where you eat it you must not sleep." On society an analogous doom—if you call it a doom—has been pronounced.

I have dwelt on this illusion of finality because one

sees it everywhere producing a dogmatic conserva-
tism, a feeling of things done and done with, than
which there is no greater obstacle to progress. You
go to a statesman and say—" This problem of the
Congested Districts is terribly pressing. You must
bring in legislation to deal with it." Then he looks
up his statute-book and says—"Congested Districts!
Oh, that question is settled; we passed an Act in
1891." It is much the same as if you were to say to
a starving man—" Dinner! Oh, you had a dinner
two months ago."

The object of politics then is order, and the object
of order is to increase the sum and improve the
quality of human life. What, we may next ask, is
the drift of current opinion as to the means that
should be used and the psychological forces that
must be put in harness in order to this end? In other
words, what political ideas has the experience of
the wonderful nineteenth century left most clearly
defined? There can be but little dispute as to
the answer. The two supreme facts, the two
shaping forces of the nineteenth century, were
Nationality and Democracy—the latter came in
direct lineage from the French Revolution, the
former brought first to full self-consciousness by the
reaction against the abstract cosmopolitanism of
'89. Look to Irish history and you will see at once
that these have been the shaping forces of the last
century of her life. But look elsewhere and you will
see the same; you will see that in this as in so many
other things Ireland has been in the main stream of
European history. The opinion of an Irish Nationalist may be suspect. I appeal, therefore, to the
authority of Professor Bury, formerly of Trinity
College, now Regius Professor of History at Cambridge. He is speaking of the impulse given to
historical studies by the upsurging of national feeling,
for, of course, a nation is before all things a spiritual

principle whose source and charter is to be found in history.

"The saying," he writes, "that the name of hope is remembrance was vividly illustrated, on a vast scale, by the spirit of resurgent nationality which you know has governed, as one of the most puissant forces, the political course of the last century and is still unexhausted. When the peoples, inspired by the national idea, were stirred to mould their destinies anew, and looking back with longing to the more distant past based on it their claims for independence or for unity, history was one of the most effective weapons in their armouries; and consequently a powerful motive was supplied to historical investigation." [1]

In Belgium, in Italy, in Hungary, in Germany, in Norway, in Poland, in Ireland, nationality has been the great formative and disruptive impulse of the nineteenth century. Whatever gloomy mood we may fall into in the struggle for autonomy we have certainly no justification for feeling lonely! There was a school of political philosophy—it still lifts here and there an antique voice—which, when it had called nationality a mere sentiment, thought that it had dismissed it from the arena of practical affairs. That habit of mind may have been excusable in the

---

[1] Bury. *An Inaugural Lecture*, 1903. P. 13. That great master of common sense and uncommon sanctity, St. Thomas Aquinas, has his lesson for modern Imperialism—"It belongs to the study of politics to know how great should be the magnitude of a state and whether it should embrace men of one or many races ; for the greatness of a state should be such that the fertility of its land is sufficient to its needs, and that it should be able to repel violent enemies. For it ought rather to be founded of one race; some oneness of nationality, involving the same manners and customs, is that which brings about friendship among citizens because of their likeness : whence states that were made up of divers nations, by reason of the dissensions that they had because of the diversity of their customs. were destroyed, since one party joined with the enemy for hatred of the other party."—*Cf.* H. C. O'Neill, *New Things and Old in St. Thomas Aquinas.*

eighteenth century. but we understand things better
now. We realize life in its concrete richness
and man as a complex of remembrances, instincts,
intuitions, and emotional needs. The historical
studies of the last century, the Romantic Movement, and the vast development of psychology,
both in formal studies and in art of every kind,
especially the novel, have rehabilitated that vast
area of consciousness which used to be dismissed
as "sentiment." There was a time when man was
conceived as an avaricious machine. If you found
anything in your mind other than calculating selfish-
ness you were outside the pale of humanity. But
now nobody need be ashamed to admit that he
detects himself in an occasional generous impulse.
Louis Kossuth was saying the other day that "it is
in active national sentiment not in political forms
that we are to look for the secret of government."
And there is not a Foreign Office in Europe but
recognizes that where there is an historic nationality,
unexpressed so far in the form of a visible state, there
is a contradiction of human nature which cannot
last. You will not ask me to analyze the idea of
Nationality. It has been discussed in this country
for the last nine or ten years with an earnestness
amounting often to fury, and nearly everything has
been said. "The nation," says Anatole France, in
a fine phrase, "is a communion of memories and of
hopes." You may well find its source in that need
for self-realization which is also, in one view, the
source of all individual morality. But that is a
notion drawn from German metaphysics, and metaphysics, if we are to believe all we read in our weekly
papers, is the unforgivable sin. But this I will say,
that if you read any one of the treatises on politics,
read at Oxford and Cambridge by the young gentlemen who afterwards come over to dragoon us, you
will find that there is not in the most exacting of

them a single test of nationality which Ireland does not satisfy. A distinctive language, a characteristic national temperament and outlook on life, a history, a sentiment of unity in the present, common memories, common interests, a geographical area large enough to constitute an independent state—is there a single one of these elements that we do not possess? If you go even further and examine the conditions demanded by these English writers to justify rebellion or disruption, adding to what has been said as to the satisfaction of national sentiment, this—I quote from Sidgwick—"Some serious oppression or misgovernment, some unjust sacrifice or grossly incompetent management of their interests, or some persistent and harsh opposition to their legitimate desires," you will find on the principles of these English writers themselves that an Irish War of Independence would be to-day justifiable if it were possible.

Side by side with Nationality stands democracy. It is impossible to define democracy; it is a principle still unrealized, an unfinished process. It has been described as "that form of social organization which tends to develop to the maximum the conscience and the responsibility of the individual citizen." This description lays stress on the central characteristic of democracy, the belief in individuality and the endeavour to foster it. To the feudalistic governing mind the citizen, or rather I should say the "subject," was an item, a something little better than a chattel, committed to the care of those whom, as the old jurists said, Providence had placed over him. The placing had, as a matter of fact, been done by the luck of circumstances. If a man had the wisdom to be born well, he sat on the necks of the masses; if he were born badly, his own neck suffered for it. Such a tyranny as this, even if it were beneficent, could not live in the atmosphere of the modern world. We have discovered that nobody is wise enough or pure enough to bear the temptation of uncontrolled power, and we are endeavouring as far as possible to remove such occasions of sin. The democratic spirit may be said to be more or less expressible in two propositions. The first is that government should rest on the active consent of the governed. It is this right and necessity of human nature that has been behind the demand for representative institutions from the beginning of the nineteenth century to the end, from the Paris barricades of 1830 and the English Reform Bill of 1832 to the Russian Revolution and the Women Suffrage movement. The second thesis of democracy is, roughly, that any one self-supporting and law-abiding citizen is, on the average, as well qualified as another for the work of government. I should prefer to put it that no citizen, or section of citizens, is as likely to conduct the government for the general benefit as the whole body of citizens acting in concert. Wherever there is a privileged class there is corruption, and a cult of sectional to the disregard of wider interests. Democracy will, of course, have its governing classes, but they will not be fortressed about with unbreachable privileges. If we now turn to Irish history it is easy to see that it is a passage from feudalism to democracy. Thus, when Mr. Michael Davitt came to write the story of the Land War, he inevitably called it *The Fall of Feudalism in Ireland*. Under the same title you might gather every stream of agitation, every Act that could be in any sense called beneficial, from the Abolition of Tithes and Catholic Emancipation to the Local Government Act. They are all parts of a process which is shifting the centre of power from privileged, arbitrary classes to responsible, representative classes. It is significant also that in that question most remote

from current politics, higher education, Democracy
has been taken for the pillar of light. Everywhere
the demand is for a democratic University; and we
mean by that not only that the fees must be low but
that the civic fervour of the institution must be high,
and that it must be a centre of creative democratic
thought.

To speak of politics is necessarily to speak of education, at least of education in citizenship. A few
words must suffice. Public opinion in this country
has made up its mind that its schools shall be places
in which love and reverence for the motherland shall
be fostered. Democracy will teach in its schools,
as well, love and reverence for the State. It is the
fashion to disbelieve in the practical value of ideas
and enthusiasms, but a democratized Ireland will
understand human nature better. The chief
channel of instruction will naturally be history,
modern history. The complete neglect of this is
the scandal of English education. History is not
only the true scientific method of approach to social
problems, it is the very substance of citizenship.

"It is of vital importance," writes Professor Bury,
"for citizens to have a true knowledge of the past
and to see it in a dry light in order that their influence on the present and future may be exerted in
right directions. . . ."

And he adds—

"It seems inevitable that, as this truth is more
fully and widely though slowly realized, the place
which history occupies in national education will
grow larger and larger."

"In France, in Germany, in America," writes the
Regius Professor of History at Oxford, Mr. Firth,
"nineteenth century history, national and European,
has a permanent place in historical studies. It is
not considered unfit for teaching or unworthy of
study; nor is it held that historical teachers or

students are incapable of studying it without displays of party feeling."[1]

So much for what I believe to be the two main ideas explanatory of contemporary Ireland as of Europe in general. One word seems to be necessary as to the limitations of politics. Politics is the science of order: it cannot take the place of the other human activities, but can only keep them in their places. Extravagant demands are sometimes made on politicians, especially in Ireland. Because they are described as "representative," people expect to find incarnate in them the whole national life from the making of shirts to the making of poetry. But politics, as such, is just as much a specialized activity as brick-laying. It is not co-extensive with life; there are vast areas of private life into which it would be tyranny for it to intrude. It does not claim, and you cannot ask it to make shirts or poetry. Its duty is to provide the conditions in which the greatest number of citizens can live happily, whether by making shirts or by making sonnets.

In what spirit should one approach the actual work of politics? I speak only for myself, but I think that one should take enthusiasm for the driving force and irony as a refuge against the inevitable disappointments. "What I need to realize," says Spencer, "is how infinitesimal is the importance of anything I can do, and how infinitely important it is that I should do it." Might not a politician choose a worse motto than that? Disillusionment is so commonly the fifth act of political agitation, mainly because of the illusive finality upon which I have touched. But a wise man soon grows disillusioned of disillusionment. The first lilac freshness of life will, indeed, never return. The graves are sealed, and no hand will open them to give us back dead comrades or dead dreams. As we

[1] C. H. Firth. *A Plea for the Historical Teaching of History.* P. 17.

14

look out on the burdened march of humanity, as we look in on the leashed but straining passions of our unpurified hearts, we can but bow our heads and accept the discipline of pessimism. Bricriu must have his hour as well as Cuchullin. But the cynical mood is one that can be resisted. Cynicism, however excusable in literature, is in life the last treachery, the irredeemable defeat. Politics, let us remember, is the province not of the second-best, as has been said, but of the second worst. We must be content, or try to be content, with little. But we must continue loyal to the instinct that makes us hope much; we must believe in all the Utopias.

If you engage in politics in Ireland, and if conditions remain as they are, certain other points must be remembered. You would do well to study the novitiate through which an idea passes before it becomes a law. It arises out of the misery, and contains in it the salvation of a countryside; the State welcomes it with a policeman's baton. It recovers; the State puts it in jail, on a plank bed, and feeds it on skilly. It becomes articulate in Parliament: a statesman from the moral altitude of £5,000 a year denounces it as the devilish device of a hired demagogue. It grows old, almost obsolete, no longer adequate; the statesman steals it, embodies it in an Act, and goes down to British history as a daring reformer. From your own side also there will be something to be borne. If you cannot agree with a colleague as to tactics, even though they be but minor tactics, he may found a paper, or write a letter, or a lyric, denouncing you to posterity as a traitor, red-handed with your country's blood. I see no help for it except to take these things as mere bye-play, decorative flourishes on the text of politics. After all there is the two-edged sword that will never fail you, with enthusiasm for one of its edges and irony for the other. However mired and weedy be the current of life there will be always joy and loyalty enough left to keep you unwavering in the faith that politics is not as it seems in clouded moments, a mere gabble and squabble of selfish interests, but that it is the State in action. And the State is the name by which we call the great human conspiracy against hunger and cold, against loneliness and ignorance; the State is the foster-mother and warden of the arts, of love, of comradeship, of all that redeems from despair that strange adventure which we call human life.

ON CROSSING THE IRISH SEA

Geography is a prudent science : but one day she will take risks, even the risk of being interesting. She will hang about the naked games and gaunt outline of places their due garment of romance. When that time comes it is not a scientist but a poet that will be chosen to evoke the spirits of hatred and tragedy, of malice and despair, of irony and disillusion which move, with unpausing haste but with no rest, over the waters of the Irish Sea.

Yet there is no outer thing that should awaken such a mood. It is a bright, even a radiant day as we clear the harbour, which in English is the King's Town, but in Irish the Fort of Laoire. The sunlight as it falls is shattered into a manifold glitter of diamonds. The soft purples and cloudy greys of the Wicklow hills shepherd you into the fold of dreams. " A pleasant land of drowsihead," as the first James Thomson would have called it, with the formal romanticism of his formal century. A vision before which the soul might well forget its anguish, and remember only its aspirations. But over it there is a shadow not of the sun's casting, the shadow of history.

A chapter of the New Geography may very well open somewhat after this fashion : Ireland is a small but insuppressible island half an hour nearer the sunset than Great Britain. From Great Britain it is separated by the Irish Sea, the Act of Union, and the perorations of the Tory party. The political philosophy of the last of these is even shallower than the physical basin of the first. Ireland is discovered from time to time by valiant journalists, mostly of a sensitive temperament. Their accounts vary. Ireland is, however, admitted by all to be unprogressive : as witness, when it is half-past twelve in London it is only five minutes past twelve in Dublin.

The people of Ireland are universally described as absolutely incapable of united action. At the same time the political machine is so monstrously efficient as to suppress all individual freedom. Observers are agreed that the Irish exhibit no tenacity of purpose or stability of character. Indeed, Froude explained the failure of Celtic Ireland to develop a native drama by this circumstance. No Irishman—he argued—has sufficient consistency of character to carry him through five acts : and you cannot put a man into a play if he insists on becoming somebody else at the end of every act. Infirm of purpose and frail of ethical fibre as she is—and all her impartial enemies concur as to the fact—Ireland has for seven centuries withstood the impact of the strongest nation in Western Europe.

Ireland has been finally conquered at least three times; she has died in the last ditch repeatedly : she has been a convict in the dock, a corpse on the dissecting-table, a street-dog yapping at the heels of Empire, a geographical expression, a misty memory. And with an obtuseness to the logic of facts which one can only call mulish, she still answers "Adsum." Her interdicted flag still floats at the mast-head, and, brooding over the symbol, she still keeps building an impossible future on an imaginary past. English parties in turn wipe her for ever off the slate of practical politics. She remains wiped off for a year or two; but as the sands slip by, the sand-built policies crumble and collapse. New battalions loom up to the right wing or the left; and the Tory Press remembers the phrase of the

Confederate General who saw victory suddenly
snatched out of his hands by Meagher's Brigade:
"There comes that damned green flag again!"

All this might seem a matter of racial pride, and
a sign of racial strength. But any Unionist can see
with half an eye—and people are Unionists precisely
because they have only half an eye to see with—that
it is mere obstinacy. It is motived by the same folly
which leads a man to waste his substance in litiga-
tion in order that he may live for all time as a
leading case. Ireland clamours incessantly for
Home Rule; she wants to sit in her own armchair
by her own fireside and mind her own business.
But the very iteration of this demand is, to any well-
conditioned mind, conclusive proof that it is not
sincere.

The unbroken triumph of the same program at
election after election shows it to be the watchword
of a purely artificial agitation. To give Ireland what
she asks for would clearly be to promote discontent
and disloyalty. In view of the peril of foreign
assault and invasion it is an indispensable part of
military tactics that Great Britain and Ireland
should be enemies, not friends. Unless Irish members of Parliament were compelled to settle the
question of English education, and English members
of Parliament compelled to settle the question of
Irish land tenure, the whole fabric of civilization
would be compromised.

It may very well be that Ireland, as a result, is
the spectre at the banquet of Empire. But was a
banquet ever dramatically complete without a
spectre? Lord Castlereagh's Act of Union must
be upheld, so much wiser is it to tie the parts of an
Empire together with a thread of formal law rather
than to let them grow together in the organic unity
which joins the main branch of a tree to the trunk.
To be sure, Home Rule does not involve the repeal

even of Lord Castlereagh's Act of Union, but it is the duty of every loyal citizen to pretend that it means complete separation. To tell the truth would shame the devil, and where would Imperialism be without the devil? As between England and Ireland, therefore,

> Let wisdom, friendship, peace, and commerce die,
> But leave us still the politician's lie.

These are, perhaps, unpardonable thoughts. It would be better to go and sit in the smoking-room, or move about amid the lively bustle of lawyers, legislators, cattle-dealers, golfers, journalists, bat-eyed tourists, and hawk-eyed commercial travellers who are doing their valiant best to annex the Irish Sea in the interest of that most greedy of all the Imperialisms, the Commonplace.

They are doing their best, but they are not succeeding. It was Uhland, I think, who paid the Rhine boatman a double fare because he had carried, unknowingly, the ghost of a dead comrade. The Company would be rich, indeed, if all the ghosts that hurry restlessly back and forward across the Irish Sea were amenable to the ticket-office! Strongbow, the first filibuster, with MacMurrough, the first traitor; Kildare, the masterful earl; Shane O'Neill going in saffron pride to greet Elizabeth as a king greets a queen; Sarsfield passing to exile and death in France; the highwaymen-bishops of the eighteenth century; Castlereagh, O'Connell, Balfour, Parnell . . . the very names are an epic and a litany of desolation.

But the deck is beginning to experiment in positions other than the horizontal. The grey, cold, sliding treachery of the sea comes out through the surface brightness. One wonders if the sea that gives empires may not take them suddenly back.

CROSSING THE IRISH SEA

At all events, I am going to be sea-sick. It will be another argument for Home Rule. "The Channel," said Grattan, using the English name for the Irish Sea, " forbids union, as the ocean forbids separation." One should be glad to be sea-sick in assertion of so slashing an epigram. To-night there will be the million globes of London to look at, gleaming through the fog like monstrous and sinister oranges in some garden of life and death. To-morrow afternoon we shall be in the House of Commons supping full of old calumnies and hatreds. But when is Ireland going to have her chance? When will voyagers, leaning on the deck-rail, catch the first purple glimpse of Wicklow with eyes innocent of political passion?

1909.

OTTO EFFERTZ:
GENTLEMAN SOCIALIST [1]

Books have their fates; and it can only be an unhappy fate that has prevented Otto Effertz' *Les Antagonismes Economiques* from achieving a brilliant position in the literature of Socialism. It is by no means his first appearance, and he is very far from being a raw revolutionary. As long ago as 1888 he made public his novel and characteristic thought in *Arbeit Und Boden*. The book was tendered as a thesis, Effertz tells us, to every University in Germany, and was rejected not *sans phrase*, but on the contrary with many pharses of violent and even scurrilous contempt by them all. The Social Democrats were no better pleased with a writer who claimed to have shattered Marxism with a single tap of his new hammer, aud none of their journals so much as reviewed *Arbeit Und Boden*. But, on the other hand, Adere writing in Conrad's great *Handworterbuch der Staatswissenschaften*, hailed Effertz as one of the few theorists of Socialism of whom the Economics of the future must take account. M. Charles Andler, who contributes a preface to *Les Antagonismes*, lectured on him in Paris. M. Adolphe Landry, whose text-book is as widely used by students in France and Switzerland as that of Gide, ranks him consistently as the peer of Marshall, Schmoller and Philipovich. Nevertheless, he hastens to add, this original German is practically unknown, and his work

[1] *Les Antagonismes Economiques.* Otto Effertz. Paris, Giard et Brière.

has been treated with contemptuous silence. Effertz himself seems to ascribe some of his ill-fortune to the fact that his first book was written in German, which is a local dialect. French is the international language of science; he will, therefore, with the aid of M. Landry, publish himself in French, and appeal to an international jury. The new departure does not seem to have succeeded. Effertz has been neither condemned nor commended by that part of the jury which sits in these countries. His book, although issued so long ago as 1906, seems hardly to have reached us. Reach us some day it must, and to bridge over the interval that separates us from a more competent performance of the task I venture to give an outline of the ideas of this strong, subtle and adventurous thinker.

Effertz is a Socialist, but he wears his red tie with a difference. He is a Socialist because Socialism is the only form of economic organization that will allow him to be a gentleman. His theory holds out to humanity the promise not of a more abundant table, but of more delicate table-manners. Remembering a fact which we are seldom suffered to forget —the existence, namely, of **Mr. Bernard Shaw**—one does not go so far as to signalize the haughtiness and daintiness of Effertz as representing a new mood in the mind of Socialism. But there is a wide gulf between the two. What to Mr. Shaw is but an elfish epigram, flung with wicked exuberance at Suburbia, is to Effertz a basal belief, an ultimate dogma, a burning passion. Under the stress of its attack many familiar lines of interpretation and of defence must be abandoned. Socialism. many of us had found comfort in saying, is a mirage of hunger. It is the economic science, or rather the economic poetry of the poor. It is the visioned Fortunate Islands of the disinherited. It is the Sociology of anæmia and defeat. If the material life of humanity is, in Kropot-

kin's phrase, the conquest of bread, then popular
Socialism is the wail of those who have been
shouldered out of the market-place with their baskets
unfilled. In the philosophy of certain of our unstrung
capitalists it is something even worse. It is the
Satanic demand that stones should be changed into
bread, in order to sustain a population swarming
beyond all bounds of prudence and self-control. "You
are pauperized by the capitalistic regime," cried out
Marx in effect to the proletariat, "In the name of
the bread of which you are defrauded, Workers of all
countries, Unite!" To Effertz this hunger-Socialism,
as one may call it, is at once unworthy and unscien-
tific. Not by bread alone do men live, but by culture
and freedom—freedom, above all, to speak the truth.
He stands for a social ideal of four dimensions; for
to *Liberté, Egalité, Fraternité* he has added another
watchword, more strident and enacting than any of
these, *Dignité*. His case against individualism is not
that it breaks the bodies of the poor with famine, but
that it defiles the souls of all men, the rich as well
as the poor. Like the aged lion in the fable he suffers
not so much from the pain as from the indignity of
the donkey's kick. Moreover, he insists, with a touch
of passion, popular Socialism is dishonest in the prospect which it holds out of illimitable harvests drawn
from an earth so limited both in area and in fertility.
His system of Pono-Physiocratic Socialism assuredly
does not mean food for all under any circumstances
of increase. It offers no unbroken round of banquets,
fit for Sybaris. Humanity, however wisely and
scientifically organized, will find itself caught perpetually between the Scylla of restrained reproduction
and the Charybdis of starvation. But if Socialism
does not promise a junketting Utopia, what, then,
does it promise? It promises, in the horoscope of
Effertz, a world in which men, while declining to be
angels, will be able to be gentlemen. Liberty—

that is to say, mere personal liberty—already approximates to its maximun in modern countries; under this rubric communized States will have no new revelation to expound. Equality cannot but widen and greaten with the growing abundance of "goods of culture" the *biens de culture* which he sets in such antithetical contrast to the *biens d'alimentation*. The general "aristocratization" of the forms of social life will bring new kingdoms under the sway of Fraternity. When we are all aristocrats it will be easy for us all to be brothers. "But the great glory of Pono-Physiocratic Socialism will centre in the complete abolition of all the indignities of the present system. A man will no longer be compelled to accept the servilities, the brutalities, the lies, the frauds, the treacheries, the whole mass of defilements and degradations which swarm in the heart of our capitalistic society, and which are forced on every member of it under the penalty of starvation for himself and his family." The rich will be redeemed from that sense of insecurity which, more even, and far more, than the appetite for actual enjoyment, is the impulse behind their unquiet lives. The worker, with trained hands eager to produce wealth for the commodity of his fellows, will no longer stand at the factory-gate begging work as an alms. The employer will be free, as now he is not free, not to exploit his employés. The shopkeeper will be free, as now he is not free, not to lie and cheat. We shall be able at last to cancel that dictum of Cicero's which is now the universal charter of the business community! *Nihil enim proficiunt institores ipsi nisi admodum mentiantur.* "It is commonly said," writes Effertz in the last of his six hundred vibrating pages, "that the social question is a belly-question, or, in more æsthetic language, a knife-and-fork question. When people preach Socialism they make their appeal to the famishing and the tatterdemalions.

25

The world is agreed that a rich man can be a Socialist only out of condescension, or political ambition, or ethical aspiration, or simply, as a joke, but never on grounds of personal interest. To accept this view is to understand very poorly the essence of Socialism. Bread and the promise of bread, there you have the weakest point of Socialism! Socialism is before all else a question of culture and dignity. When we preach Socialism it is to the dignity of mankind that we must primarily appeal. *Gentlemen of all countries, Unite !* "

Such is the ethos and inspiration of this strange book. If Effertz brings a new temper to Socialism, he also brings a new theory. He himself is indeed urgent to disclaim all originality; his only gift is that of fertilizing the neglected commonplaces of Economics. The professors of that science have not understood the value of their analyses; like Balaam's ass they speak great words without understanding what they speak. They have a Cyclopean power to quarry huge blocks of stone, but the lyre of Apollo does not sound among them to uprear the walls of Troy. The fundamental truths of economic science are as old as Petty and Bernouilli: they are expounded in every rudimentary manual of the subject. But there is a curious flaw in such expositions. The basal laws and problems are formulated indeed, but not " sacramentally," not *in sede materiae.* This flaw Effertz will correct, and therein lies his sole originality. His only other novelty is a novelty of arrangement. He introduces into Sociology the dramaturgical principle. The fact of antagonism of interest between individual and individual, between the individual and society, between the present and the future, being ultimate, we shall do well to cast our treatment of it into the literary form most appropriate to such an order of reality. This is obviously the drama, for the essential note of drama is the conflict of wills. The first section of such a Sociology will correspond to the Intrigue, the delineation of interests. The second will exhibit as Catastrophe the clash in actual life of one economic interest with another. In the third section, analogous to the Intermediate Chorus, the writer will proceed to an ethical criticism of a conflict, the economic mechanism of which has thus been exhibited. This merges into the Denouement, a discussion of the legal and political arrangements by which the lesion of higher interests may as far as possible be avoided; and our drama of humanity culminates in the Final Chorus, with a summary of those antagonisms which enquiry shows to be irreconcilable, and lamentations over the incurable evils of life. The five divisions may be rendered into more usual nomenclature as the sciences of Pure Economics and Applied Economics, the arts of agitation and of statesmanship, with a finale of philosophy. The adequate handling of this five-fold analysis gives ample play to the rich and subtle mind of Effertz. Mathematician, psychologist, pioneer, dandy, and admirable classicist, he has a sense of style and a feeling for literature unequalled by any German thinker since Schopenhauer. Differential equations rub shoulders with dashing epigrams. We plod with difficult steps through pages of curves and graphs, and then suddenly the wilderness of x and y blossoms like the rose. Effertz is, as I have said, classical in his literary loyalties; and nothing could exceed the wicked delight with which he shows us all political economy lying folded up in a couplet of Goethe or in three threadbare hexameters of Horace. A copious creator of new terms, he invents one to characterize himself. It is the custom of authors to publish books in order to educate others: he publishes, however, solely to educate himself. He is, in scientific matters, a pure *égosophe*, who expounds his thought in order that it may be criticized and thereby made perfect. And if he refuses to influence opinion he is even more urgent to repel the notion that his theory can lead to revolutionary action. University professors—whose attitude towards burning questions is ever that of a cat towards hot soup—have ignored him because they believed that a writer who laid such emphasis on the disharmonies and antagonisms of economic life must necessarily be a disturber of the peace. Such an idea is absurd. Effertz has a particular aversion and contempt for bombs and barricades. "It is only a partial knowledge of social antagonisms that can lead men to desire a revolution. The best way to make revolutions unpopular, and to create a sedative temper of reform, is to furnish a complete picture of these antagonisms." An agitator who has heard of only a single "class-war" is in danger of believing that the source of this class-war may be swept away for ever, and humanity definitively redeemed with the flame and fanfare of one great upheaval. It is an illusion that still exists, and that must be banished. What can be more potent to banish it than a Sociology which exhibits economic disharmony not as an isolated and destructible fortress of privilege, but as a vast labyrinth co-extensive with society? For men who respect their intellects only one honourable path is open, the path of peaceful reform.

After such an overture the fundamental ideas of Effertz must seem bare and simple. His system is characterized by M. Andler as the most vigorous attempt ever made to constitute a science of Pure Economics. By this term he understands the analysis and interpretation of those economic facts which exist independently not alone of the special juridical system of any state, but also of the processes of exchange. Denuded then to its ultimate skeleton, economic life manifests itself as a drama, which, like the French stage, has its "eternal triangle." Land, labour, and consumption are the three apex-points about which all economies function, be they primitive or advanced. The collaboration of labour with land to produce a utility is the foundation of all systems. Every good contains a certain quantity of labour and a certain quantity of land, but no good contains anything else. In the metaphor of Petty, labour is the father, and land is the mother of all wealth. This analysis of production is, we may agree with Effertz, the most worn and battered common-place of all the text-books. Every theorist has seen it, but hardly one has consistently believed it. To anybody who grasps it steadily the dictum on which Marx builds his whole system comes as an amazing counter-sense. " If, then, we leave out of consideration the use-value of commodities," writes Marx in the indispensable first chapter of *Das Kapital*, " they have only one common property left, that of being products of labour."

Marxian Socialism is by this principle, the Ponocratic illusion, involved in strange absurdities. It would, for instance, necessitate the exchange of three or four bullocks for one good book; since the "labour certificates," which are to be the measure of exchange, would show that the named quantities of these very diverse products embodied equal quantities of labour. The ratio between literature and beef might indeed be even more favourable to the former on the score of the superior skill of the labour concerned. Obviously commodities have another common property; each of them embodies a certain quantity of land. In any given process of consumption—say that of bread—we bite the dust in an unsuspected sense, we are veritable eaters of earth. And the earth being very far from infinite this fact is of dominant importance in all economies. Effertz confesses with surprise that for once literature fails him. While every language has a phrase like *manger du travail* or *manger de la sueur* in currency, he cannot find either in the verses of the learned or in the proverbs of the people any locution such as *manger de la terre*. He coins it forthwith, with an explanation which affords such a good example of what one may term the conscientious nastiness of his science that it ought to be quoted here in its more or less decent veil of French. "Pour éviter les malentendus grossiers, je dois faire remarquer que si je dis 'manger de la sueur, de la terre,' je ne parle pas en *chimiste*; je ne parle pas de *géophagie*, et je ne fais pas allusion à la sueur matérielle qui est mélangée chimiquement avec presque toutes les denrées coloniales. Je parle en économiste et je pense à cette sueur et à cette terre qui sont renfermées métaphysiquement dans les biens."

The relation of the three elements engaged may be expressed in mathematical or pseudo-mathematical form. The final unknowns, positive and negative, of economic calculation are x = the utilities consumed by an individual in the unit of time, and y = the labour expended by the individual in the unit of time in the acquisition of these utilities. In calculating the curves, in which he forecasts the future of mankind, Effertz employs an armoury of some forty auxiliary symbols. On the technical side they constitute, indeed, so large a part of his work that his use of them ought to be illustrated. Designating, then, by w the utility of a good, by a the quantity of labour, and by b the quantity of land embodied in it, we are able to formulate an absolute value, not dependent on any special regime or even on exchange. This absolute value varies with the quotient, satisfaction : sacrifice. The productivity of any exploitation, or more generally of any form of economic organization being represented by p, we arrive forthwith at the formula $p = \dfrac{w}{a + b}$. To maximise p, by weighting a and b with appropriate coefficients, and by understanding the psychological determinants of w, is the task laid upon all future governments. In discussing further the relation of a and b, Effertz makes his sole claim to originality. He has introduced two new principles into Sociology, the principle of conflict and the principle of incitation. Passing by the first of these for a moment, I shall try to explain the second. All previous economists have treated the two factors of production as co-operating forces, the resultant of which is represented by a diagonal. But in point of fact, Effertz argues, the true relation is that of an inciting factor, labour, to an incited factor, land; and the economy which results corresponds not to the diagonal of the parallelogram of forces, but to what he styles a *décrochement*. One who is not an initiate in the Higher Mathematics had best seek refuge in the original "La production est le procès par lequel l'incitant travail décroche une valeur d'usage en incitant de la terre." The whip, he says, in a deliberately ludicrous image, is the inciting, the cab-horse the incited factor: you may manage with a smaller horse by using a larger whip; but no extension of the whip, even to infinity, will compensate for the total disappearance of the horse. This novel terminology and the mathemical exercises by which it is supplemented are not much dwelt upon by M. Landry. But it is difficult to see how any specialist in Mathematical Economics can, with due regard to his own competence, ignore the first section of *Les Antagonismes*. The third of the primordial elements w, or the utility of goods, has for Effertz found its final

formulation in Daniel Bernouilli's *De Mensura Sortis,*
published in 1738. Bernouilli's law contains for him
all the truth and none of the confusion of the "marginal utility" theory of the Austrians. Analogous
to the law of Weber and Fechner in Psycho-Physics,
it asserts that the subjective satisfaction produced
by the objective consumption of a given quantity of
any good is in inverse ratio to the quantity of the
good already consumed. Furnished with this key
to the variation of needs and desires, and with the
coefficients representing skill, fertility and the like
which qualify a and b in any concrete case, Effertz
undertakes rather vainly to make his equations as
accurate as those of Physics. Before passing from
his elaborate analysis of exchange one ought. perhaps, to signalize the invention of the term *monoone,*
or monoony, to designate a form of unilateral competition, which is the obverse of monopoly, and is
almost as common. One seller confronting many
buyers gives us a phenomenon of monopoly, one
buyer confronting many sellers gives us a phenomenon of monoony. For the rest it is, perhaps,
enough to say that in Pure Economics Effertz touches
no question that he does not freshen; his discussions
cast novel, though perhaps distorting, lights on the
whole sub-structure of the science.

Every good is, as all economists have noted, a
synthesis of labour with land, but the proportions in
which these elements are combined vary over a very
wide range. On closer scrutiny there emerges a fact
which controls the whole future of humanity, whether
under Socialism or under Individualism. It is this:
generally speaking those goods which require for
their production much land and comparatively little
labour are articles of food, *biens d'alimentation,*
and those which require much labour and comparatively little land are instruments of culture or luxury,
biens de luxe ou de culture. An instance already cited

32

will serve here also—the contrast, namely, between bullock and books. The variations of the quotient— $\frac{b}{a}$ involve many important consequences. The first of these is enunciated by Effertz in what he calls the non-transformability or non-interchangeability of forms of production. Any given form of production, that is to say, cannot in general be transformed into any other, but only on condition that the quotient $b:a$ of the two is approximately the same. Effertz in his exposition distinguishes, but not quite clearly, between quantitative and qualitative variations of the land engaged in production. Judas, he points out, gave utterance to very feeble though very popular Economics in complaining that the precious ointment had not been converted into food for the poor. In this case the absurdity is obvious. Under our system of exchange you can substitute one commodity for another, and transfer the sin, if there be a sin, of luxury to somebody else; but by no chrematistic magic can you tranform the first product into something so different in nature as the second. The more plausible fallacy, however, is that which regards, not products, but branches of production as interchangeable. This illusion beclouds the prophetic vision alike of the Malthusian pessimists and the Socialistic optimists. The former imagine that when the pressure of over-population begins, every other branch of production will be transformed into the production of food, and that consequently the debacle to which mankind, increasing at its present rate, is in their view irredeemably committed will have famine only as its last phase. All culture, all luxury will have been thrown to the wolves before their fangs come abreast of the sleigh. The reply of Effertz is that if such a crisis is to come, it will not end but begin with hunger. The one category of goods of which there need never be a scarcity is that category which demands a great deal of labour, but little land—namely, goods of culture. The Socialists also, when confronted with a familiar criticism, reply in terms of the same fundamental error. Under your Socialism, says a critic, suppose that I call to your communistic store with a bunch of labour-notes and ask fer a bottle of bock. They have no bock, but they offer me a copy of Marx, of which there is a superabundance! What then? Nothing simpler, reply the Socialists. You write to the Minister of Production, Department of Transformations: he gives instructions to divert some labour from printing and publishing to agriculture and brewing; and next season there will be no shortage of bock. But No! says Effertz, you are working on a groundless assumption. You can transform a production of *Das Kapital* into one of *Harmonies Economiques*, or one of bock into one of milk or cider. But you cannot transmute a production, in which very little land and a great deal of labour are required, into one that demands very little labour but a great deal of land. Ponocratic Socialism will discover in such a juncture, that by founding its currency solely on one of the primordial elements, it has exhausted the other, it will have eaten up imprudently its whole allowance of land.

In this reiterated sentence we come upon Effertz' reason for positing antagonism of interest as an ultimate and unchangeable factor in human society. *Homo homini lupus* is the law that emerges from every analysis of consumption. Who touches this book, said Whitman, touches a man. But with Effertz to eat a potato is to eat a man, or at least the potential existence of a man. He finds remorse and embarrassment mixed as ingredients in every plate of soup. " I cannot get rid of the thought that in eating I am destroying one of my fellows. I say

34

to myself, indeed, that not to eat would be to destroy myself, and that I am worth as much as another. But I eat it with disgust, as if I had found a hair in it." Labour we must also consume, and so far forth every consumer is forced to "exploit" somebody. But at least there need be no remorse if one pays his score by furnishing to society as much productive labour as he consumes. In the world in which we live this is a difficult counsel. So many pleasant commodities, so many lucrative productions are possible to us only on condition that others shall be given over to death, servitude, or dishonour. You accept, for instance, the Arab proverb that the Earthly Paradise is to be found on horseback. But since a horse consumes as much earth as would sustain three men, to keep a horse is to murder a family, to keep a stable is to maintain a sort of perpetual massacre. Nor is it to be supposed that this sombre halo attaches only to articles of luxury. Fishers must, indeed, be drowned in order that a rich woman may wear a rope of pearls, but fishers must also be drowned in order that a beggar may eat a herring. The shop-girl, who wears imitation lace, and the duchess, who wears real lace, condemn some of their sisters to slavery and exploitation with the same ruthless certainty. As for dishonour, society has grown itself a very rhinoceros hide of hypocrisies to protect us from the edged and miserable facts which cannot be denied. You must not let your right hand know what your left hand does, nor whisper in your drawingroom what you thunder in your office. Public opinion agrees to equate honour with income, and to employ between friends the suaver synonym. There is a nice gradation in these things :—

> Mein Sohn, o lern das Leben kennen !
> Gar vornehm ist es Schnaps zu brennen ;
> Bedenklich schon ihn zu verkaufen,
> Und ganz-erbärmlich ihn zu—saufen.

If there is, however, a certain ultimate antagonism, woven into the fabric of reality, there are many
secondary antagonisms which result merely from the
property basis on which contemporary societies agree
to stand. In his social pathology Effertz proceeds.
in his own characteristic way, upon certain ideas of
Rodbertus. Like the latter he finds the main source
and cause of economic disharmonies in the almost
universal clash between *rentabilité* and *productivité*.
Under our regime of exchange the production of
commodities is governed not by the needs of men,
but by the fluctuations of the market. The individual
producer obtains his maximum income in many cases
not by maximising but, on the contrary, by restricting
production. The earlier strategy of the speculator
in this regard was brutal and elementary: it consisted in the material destruction of products. The
lesson taught by the Sibyl—namely, that a monopolist
can exact the same price for three as for twelve
articles—was well learned by Rome. The manipu-
lation of the grain market, by the burning of
superabundant supplies, was so commonly practised
as to evoke legislation providing severe penalties for
this *crimen dardanariatus*, as it was named after
Dardanarius, its inventor. The Middle Ages found
themselves still confronted by the *dardanarius*, and
burned him alive when occasion offered; and Effertz
asserts that even to-day in the East the rice market,
and in certain Dutch colonies the spice market, are
subject to the same gross and barbaric methods.
Modern speculation is more subtle and more effective :
it understands how to hold back, and hold up supplies, without destroying them. No consumer can
stretch out a hand without coming against one mesh
or another of the network of *quasi-dardanariatus* in
which it has enveloped the world. This is the
deepest disharmony, but there are many others.
Present is at war with future : the wasteful technique

of American agriculture, for instance, maximises production for one generation, but leaves an exhausted soil to the next. There is a war between true interest and imaginary interest, even for a man who has deliberately chosen egotism for his guide: even on his own low plane he is continually deluded by our chrematistic, modern habit of mind. Every man, labouring under higher ideals, bears about in his soul a far fiercer war between the economic and the gamic virtues. He has two soul-sides, one to cheat, exploit, and subjugate the world with in order that the other may shower luxury and advancement on his household. The only variation is between that struggle in which the object is destruction, and that in which the object is domination. Competition between one employer and another, or one worker and another within the same trade, supplies an example of the first. Its motto is: *Des einen Brod ist des anderen Tod,* bread to one man is death to another. Conflicts between a capitalist and a labour syndicate exemplify the second. The watchword in this case is: *Des einen Brod ist des anderen Noth,* one man's plenty is another man's famine. In one or other of these forms the fact of antagonism is written in a flaming and sinister scribble over the whole map of our modern economy. The masters of that economy, sniffing the gold coins in their palms, echo the Cæsar's *non olet.* But that is a judgment of chemistry, not of ethics. To a mind once shaken out of our habitual, dogmatic drowse all money appears tainted, every sovereign stinks. We have created a civilization of great and cruel splendour, and written over its gate: *No gentleman need apply.*

Out of this base labyrinth there is only one clew that can be safely followed, that of Pono-Physiocratic Socialism. The weakness of popular Socialism by no means lies in its supposed inability to maintain production at the maximum. In comparison with our present industrial system it offers a clear superiority, consequent on the removal of all conflict between *rentabilité* and *productivité*, between lucrative and productive exploitation. The true and fatal flaw is to be found in the proposed mechanism of exchange. This flaw is now for the first time removed. The impossibility of the Marxian labour-certificates having been demonstrated, Effertz proceeds to outline what Andler styles a bimetallism of land and labour. Under this system all articles are to be double-ticketed, so as to show their cost in land and their cost in labour; and no article is to be sold in exchange for wage-certificates of one kind only. In issuing land certificates, which are, so to say, a free bonus given to the worker in addition to his labour-certificates, the State will keep steadily before its mind the territorial area at its command, and will be able to control the increase of population and to avert famine. It will be able further, without invading the personal liberty of the citizens, to impel their labour, as the need may be, towards production for the sake of culture or production for the sake of sustenance. The general effect will be to equalize the distribution of the necessaries of physical life. This will provide—in accordance with the only defensible statement of the materialistic interpretation of history—the negative conditions of culture. Its positive reality and richness and the actual distribution of *biens de culture* will follow a law determined by the genius and ideals of individual intellects. On the material side Pono-Physiocratic Socialism will give equality to the equal, on the mental side it will give inequality to the unequal. This accords with all our experience. Even in present conditions a capitalist consumes little more land than a workman; like Napoleon he can dine only once in a day. His main consumption is labour, his main motive is ostentation, his main instrument of acquisition is mere money and the chrematistic illusion. His psychology differs organically from that of the workman. "The worker perishes when he no longer has soup to eat. The capitalist perishes when he no longer has Sèvres ware in which to offer soup to his parasites." Under the system of Effertz both of them will have soup, since all men need soup; as for the Sèvres, it can only be acquired by a citizen who is able to supply society with labour as skilled and intellectual as that which produced it. A larger hope for all unfolds itself in the consideration that in a progressive nation, while the curve of goods of sustenance no sooner climbs to its maximum than it is dragged down again by growing weight of population, the curve of goods of culture ought to maintain a continuous ascent approximating to a straight line. Therein lies the rule of life of the honourable, and the ambition of the wise. The luxury of a Lassalle, little though it may dim the brilliance of that splendid and reckless spirit, compromises the whole cause of Socialism. If you would be master of the future you must rather choose for your pattern, Spinoza, who built his great basilica of metaphysics on twopence a day.

Effertz, with an amiable weakness not infrequent among his countrymen, admits that he may well be regarded as the Kant of Sociology. As Kant opened a new path between dogmatism and scepticism by posing sacramentally and *in sede materiae* the question of the limits of attainable human knowledge, so Effertz, by posing in the same solemn fashion the question of the limits of attainable human happiness, opens a new path between optimism and pessimism. He founds the Critical School of Sociology. The fashion in which he answers his own question has already been indicated. But in believing himself to be impartial he is deeply wrong : his place is with the pessimists. No other judgment is possible to any one who has toiled through the grey, chill, and intricate galleries of his thought. In his vision, even the light counterfeits a gloom. Asking with Faust : Was kann die Welt mir wohl gewähren ? he answers with Faust ! Enthehren sollst du, sollst enthehren. With Schiller he declares that life is error and illusion, and that only in death do we lay hold on reality. " Humboldt writes somewhere that the greatest happiness possible to any human being is to be born an imbecile, since only an imbecile can live without coming to understand the truth of things. This observation holds good in general, but it is specially applicable to the study of society. Those who have lifted the veil of sociological truth, those who have eaten the fruit of the tree of Sociology, can never again be happy. A veil was thrown over the image of Saïs, because that image represented—Truth." It would be easy, and quite true, to say that the pessimism of Effertz results from a mistake of fact, taken too seriously. High authorities can be cited to show that the menace of famine, which obsesses him, is so remote as not properly to enter into the present thought of humanity. It would be easy, and quite idle, to observe that the man who analyses is lost, and that the only counsel of happiness is to feel feelings and enjoy enjoyments. Optimism and pessimism are, perhaps, primary colours of mind, positive and negative polarities which we can only accept without understanding. They are, it may be, the day and the night of the human spirit, established for an eternal contrast and counterchange ; and Effertz fulfils the destiny of a man born under the sun's eclipse. Optimist or pessimist matters little in a life marshalled under the trumpet of duty : your emotions are your own, and you are free to feel that all the problems that beset us are insoluble on condition that you help to solve them. To this task Effertz has bent a strong and subtle mind. While he has not made Socialism more tolerable he has at least made it more acute, and his contribution to Pure Economics possesses a high value, not at all dependent on his practical creed. *Les Antagonismes* with its keen sense of the fundamental, its harsh courage, its store of rich and strange observation, cannot fail to count for something, nor can any economist afford to pass by in complete silence the system of Otto Effertz, Gentleman Socialist.

1910.

ON WRITTEN
CONSTITUTIONS

I agree that it is most unfortunate that we should have to introduce at any time a written provision into an unwritten constitution.
(Hear, hear.)—Mr. Haldane in the House of Commons.

Mr. Haldane is a formidable rather than a popular
speaker, an authority but not an inspiration. It is,
of course, a question of personality. He looks like
a composite photograph of six German philosophers,
with a varnish of Renan, and that is not a bad
beginning. But that singular voice of his which
comes piping out of rotundity is too thin, light, and
metaphysical ever to be a trumpet of democracy.
It is in vain that all men concede him the aureole
of omniscience. It is in vain that the House rejoices
to see in his radiant presence a refutation of the
epigram in which Ecclesiastes declares that increase
of knowledge means increase of sorrow. He stirs
the imagination to pleasant pictures. To me, he is
always some friar of the Ingoldsby Legends lilting
black-letter Statutes and Gothic ideologies to the
music of a penny whistle.

But with all that blithe omniscience, he remains
formidable rather than effective. His speech of the
other night, from which the sentence at the head of
this essay is quoted, ran counter to the sense of
his own party. It was delivered with a sort of taut
rectitude, and received in, what is called, courteous
silence. But that particular sentence was greeted,
as it always is greeted in the House of Commons,
with a regular musketry-rattle of " Hear, hears." It
seems to me not inapt to the times to analyse these
" Hear, hears."

WRITTEN CONSTITUTIONS

This prejudice against written constitutions is, beyond doubt, one of the best-established superstitions of English politics. Every law student, nurtured on that masterpiece of romance, Dicey's *Law of the Constitution*, has in his day written essays in praise of the spontaneous and elastic system under which we are supposed to live. He has been taught to believe that every Continental jurist looks with envy and despair from his own miserable paper-guarantees of freedom to this organic body which has grown with the growth, and strengthened with the strength of the British nation. And somehow it is suggested that, as Lohengrin had to disappear on being forced to give his name and address, so the magic of the English constitution would disappear if it were written down. Hence these " Hear, hears."

Now I wish to submit, and by no means respectfully, that this traditional view is little better than stately nonsense. Continental jurists do not envy England. They say : " Truly, my friend, the British constitution would, without doubt, be admirable. But, alas ! it does not exist." The writing down of custom and practice is not a misfortune, but a most happy achievement. And in dealing with England you are dealing not with an unwritten, but with a badly written, constitution. This last point demonstrates itself. How do you go about to prove the provisions of your unwritten constitution ? By an appeal to Magna Charta. But Magna Charta is a document, not a custom. By an appeal to the " Indemnity of Parliament " of 1407, to the Resolution of 1640, to the Resolution of 1671, to the Resolution of 1678. These are strange elements to appear in an unwritten constitution. Take away the scribe, the Commons clerk, and the printer, and neither Indemnity nor Resolution would exist or operate to-day.

The amusing truth is that this myth of an

unwritten English constitution, with its whole virtue residing in the fact that it was unwritten, was invented by an Irishman. Edmund Burke invented it because it happened to give him a good debating-point against the French Revolution, But why should our radical legatees of the French Revolution cling to it as tenderly as to a memory of their childhood? They ought, on the contrary, to say: "Since so much has been written, let us write the rest, and write it clearly."

One has no difficulty in believing that Simon de Montfort had a certain weakness for unwritten constitutions, but that was only because, in all probability Simon de Montfort did not himself write or read with any comfort. But the whole colour of the times has changed. Writing, which in those far-off days was the special magic of a small caste, is the common form of modern democracy. Before the Print Age, to rely on documents rather than on custom would have been esoteric. Since the Print Age, to rely on custom rather than on documents is mere antiquarian pedantry.

The two opposite mistakes have this in common: they are, both of them, modes of keeping government separated from the dust, the tumult, and the heartiness of common life. That is the aim of Toryism; and Tory constitutionalists like Mr. Dicey are singing in the key of their policy when they sing the praises of tacit agreements, accepted conventions, and the other elements of unwritten constitutions. But when Mr. Haldane joins the chorus, he is, I submit, engaging in high treason against those two born Progressives, the pen and the printing-press. The pen in old days was the jousting lance; the Press in these days is the armoured Dreadnought of Radicalism.

There is nothing peculiarly English in this dread of documents. It is a characteristic of all primi-

tive societies. You have one form of the superstition in the Arab who expects to be cured—
and often is cured!—by rolling a piece of paper with
a doctor's prescription on it up into a ball and
swallowing it. You have another in the contemporary farmer who cannot be induced to keep accounts.
He prefers to work on an unwritten constitution,
"like his father before him." The result is that when
he gets to the Bankruptcy Court he has to go without even the poor consolation enjoyed by the rest of
us—namely, an exact knowledge of how he got there.
Within the field of law itself the whole movement is
from custom and the spoken word to Statute and the
written word. If not, why is it that when you have
made a contract over the telephone you immediately
dictate a letter embodying its terms, and send it off
by the evening post ?

The same thing holds true of industry and commerce. Everywhere the formula, the diagram, the
blue drawing, the visible, written, permanent word
have triumphed. In commerce, to take an example
from history, Venice owed her greatness partly, no
doubt, to geography, but largely also to book-keeping.
Venice held the Golden East in fee because her
merchants were the first to abandon the old unwritten
constitution of hand-to-mouth trading in favour of
double-entry book-keeping. Her flaming pageant,
in which life and art mingled their frontiers insepar-
ably, was organized by the glorious clerks who wrote
down her accounts in a large, legible hand. The
splendour of Titian was nothing more than the
flowering of a ledger.

Toryism has imagined the vague, unwritten regime,
which is its opportunity, as a natural and organic
growth. But change the image. Say instead that
it is like music-hall patter, made up as one goes
along. Say that it is like an extempore speech, and
that extempore speeches are always bad. Say that

it is, so far, the mere nebula and protoplasm of freedom to which this age must give clear articulation and definite form. All the tides are flowing in that direction. Within the last ten years England has made constitutions for Australia, for the Transvaal, for the Orange River, for United South Africa. It is time that she made a Constitution for herself, guarding liberty with a quantitative formula. And that will help us all to join in making a Constitution for Ireland.

1910.

BODY *v.* SOUL

Francis Thompson is known to us as perhaps the most wastefully abundant imagination of the present day. He has taken the sun for patron, and all his poetry welters with the sun's fervour and fecundity. They are in his very style and wordy vesture, that imperial style of his into which he has adopted purple Latinities as aptly as the Church has adopted the stateliness of the Roman paenula. But we must be on our guard against his splendours; we must not let them betray us into construing his work as mere literature. One fears that some delusion of the kind has captured many of those who praise him. They have praised him as a lord of language, a tyrant of images, and it has hardly occurred to them to search out the spirit behind the grandiose ceremonial. It is possible, it is even certain, that many readers of such a poem as *The Hound of Heaven* have exulted in its tidal flux without taking it to mean anything in particular. But that is not the colour of the poet's own mind. He has never spoken for the sake of speaking, but always because he had something to say. "What, after all," says Brunetière, "is poetry but a metaphysic made manifest through sensible images?" Great poetry surely is; if not a criticism, it is a vision of life, of the structure and basal laws of life. When a man's eyes have been once opened the common day flames and vibrates with bladed chariots. The most insignificant object or experience stands vested with endless relations, or rather there is nothing that can any longer be called insignificant. The lightest caprice

47

of love has its metaphysical implications, and to salute a primrose is to proclaim a philosophy. We all understand this, or at least our wise memories do, in their choice of what to reject and what to retain. That poetry alone lives in us which is so great that it has forgotten to be poetic. We think of its sincerity, its absolute truth, or what other word we grasp at to describe what cannot be described, not of its technical deftness or even mastery. A something has come upon and transmuted it, it shines with the light of glorification. Francis Thompson has always understood this. Painting the veil of life with colours dipped out of the rising and the setting of the sun, he has known that nothing was of any account save what lay behind the veil, the spiritual interpretation that can never be wholly expressed. Earth and all the business of earth have been to him at once a spectacle and a sacrament. His work belongs less to literature than to mysticism. Do we not think of it as of something essentially hieratic, full of costly spices, brought out of the East, of figured chasubles, and full of the mysteries of grace?

It was necessary to bring all this back to mind in order to induce the mood in which the little book before us must be considered.[1] For it is no casual bye-product of the writer's mind, as might possibly be suspected from its appearance in a series, very aptly called " The Science of Life Series." It is thorough Thompson. The author has simply picked out a certain drift of thought which lies implicit in all his poetry, and supported it by instances and considerations drawn from many quarters. Such a prosifying of intuitions has an interest quite apart from its subject matter. It helps to dispel the notion that poetry comes irresponsibly out of the

[1] *Health and Holiness.* A Study of the Relations between Brother Ass, the Body, and his Rider, the Soul. By Francis Thompson.

air, and not reflectively out of the stuff of everyday ;
and it shows the supreme reasonableness, the gross
commonsense, of mysticism. But we must not stray
aside, though it were, like the Crusaders, to capture
Constantinople. The book is simply a brief srudy
of the terms prescribed by ascetical tradition to
keep the peace between those ally-enemies, Soul
and Body, with a plea for a new Concordat to meet
new conditions. Mr. Thompson is on the side of
the body; in the interests of the spirit itself he
demands a more clement regime and never did
cause rejoice in an abler advocate. He has the
incommunicable gift of the phrase, the phrase that
is like a key-stone to knit together fabrics of experience, like a cavalry-charge to drive an argument
home. The task of summarizing him is therefore
extremely difficult, and I shall try to do no more
than convey in general terms the point of view from
which he justifies and ennobles Brother Ass.

In so far as he pleads for a mildening of the
discipline of the religious orders we have no concern
to follow him. Some have already relaxed, others
are in the train of relaxing their first austerity ; and
there must always be some that will preserve it to
be a refuge for those virile and passiouate souls who
thirst for brimmed measures of expiation, and are
able to bear them. " The weltering problem of
secular religion," is, as the writer says, quite enough
for us. Take the unheroic, modern man, with all
his aches and pains, and ask what is religion to
make of him. What ascesis must be adopted so
as to make him an instrument capable of divine
melodies ?

For the soul is to the body, as the breath is to the flute,
Both together make the music, either marred and all is mute.

And first, how does this modern body stand in its
internal self ? Surely, as Mr. Thompson says, it

E   49

is "an etiolated body of death." The nerves of
the twentieth century have gone bankrupt. Life
has become too elaborate and too exacting for them;
they have gone down under the iron rod of erudition
and the whip of practical labour. The age's characteristic cry is the cry of disease. Men go abont
making public confession of their ailments, or,
delivered from them, gather disciples to the gospel
of the perfect digestion. Patent medicines are in-
vested by their sellers with an all-sufficiency that
would have made Paracelsus blush for his modesty.
Commissions are appointed to enquire into Physical
Degeneration. The army authorities cry out that it
is impossible to find recruits who are even good
enough to be food for powder. Schools for Physical
Culture multiply, in England at least, with a rapidity
which illustrates, as even the three hundred religious
sects did not, that great people's genius for dissension.
No alert man has time to consider anything, save
what he shall eat and what he shall drink, and
wherewith he shall be clothed. We go about
creepily conscious of the iniquities of our livers, and
of the freaks of our subliminal selves. For alike
from the physical side and from the mental come
physicians, Christian Scientists, Hypnotists, Will-
Developers, Faith-Healers—it is beyond human
power to name the innnmerable brood. There is
an association in America, whose members are
pledged to spend an hour every week wishing fellow-
members good health and good fortune. The annual
subscription is only a dollar, and this will be returned
if within a year one does feel appreciably better, and
obtain a "rise."

It is a Danse Macabre, with an interfusion of the
crudest farce. But it is difficult to find much relief
in the humorous mask of it. That mask drops off,
and abandons us to something not far from terror.
Cerebral physiology, psychiatry as it is pursued, not

in shilling treatises, but in the schools, begins to disclose more fully the interrelations of mind and body; and the awful delicacy of the instrument on which we play, its complex fallibility comes near overwhelming us. It is something we have rea about in the text-books, how "a brain-fever changed a straight-walking youth into a flagitious and unprincipled wastrel. And recently," adds Mr. Thompson, " we had the medically-reported case of a model lad, who, after an illness, proved a liar and a pilferer." Or it is somebody we have known, flaming, impetuous, who was pushing on by forced marches to his goal; and then his outraged body turned traitor, and the world had come to an end for him. The brain has become the theatre of a tragedy which is continually renewed. " How remote we are," cries out Guyau in his poignant speech "from the naïve perception of the primitive world which located the soul in the breast, or, it may be, even in the stomach! It is, as we kuow, the braiu that thinks, it is the brain that suffers, it is the brain that throbs with the torment of the Unknown, it is the brain that is signed with the sacred wound of the Ideal, it is the brain that quivers under the beak of the winged and ravening intellect. In the mountains of Tartary the traveller sometimes sees a strange animal leap panting by in the greyness of the dawn. The great eyes, strained wide with suffering, are those of an antelope; but as the hoofs thud by, the ground beneath trembling like a heart in agony, two huge wings are seen wildly beating to and fro above the head which they seem to lift up and on. The antelope dashes madly down the winding valley, leaving a red trail on the rocks, staggers, falls, and the two great wings soar up from the antlers, disclosing the eagle which, with talons sunk deep in the skull, had been devouring the brain and the life of the antelope." The parable would come with a

familiar air to Mr. Thompson, for it is obvious that
either from great sympathy or from sharp experience
he knows all these secrets of the prison-house. He
is cognisant of lives that have become a dread
Rosary in which there are only sorrowful mysteries.
Has not he himself written of one who

> Paced the places infamous to tell,
> Where God wipes not the tears from any eyes?

He comes in this book to write of these things in
plain prose, to consider how they can be wrought up
into religion, and whether sanctity may not have in
it a tonic quality. The demand which he makes of
the life, whether of the saint or of the rest of us, is
simply that it shall live. " Holiness energises. The
commonest of common taunts is that of 'idle monks,'
'lazy saints,' and the like. But, most contrary to
that superficial taunt, a holy man was never yet an
idle man . . . . and a saintly could never be an
effete world." But I could not do justice to his
thought without quoting in full those proud, trumpet-
pages, in which he celebrates the " incidental greatness" of the saints when they turned half-disdainfully
to secular pursuits—the lyric majesty of the Prophets,
the Confessions of Augustine, the Hymn to the Sun
of St. Francis of Assisi, the incomparable prose of
St. Francis de Sales. The problem with us all, then,
is to evoke from the federation of body and soul the
fullest stream of energy, and to turn it to the highest
ends; and to do this we must respect the laws and
the limitations of both. The body is like a wick
immersed in the oil of the spirit—it was Heine's
image—and "though the oil can immensely energize
and prolong the life of the wick, it is on that cor-
poreal wick, after all, that the flame of active energy
depends." How then is our end to be accomplished?
Not by the heroic maceration of the first or the
middle ages. The ascesis of these days, transmitted

to us in the discipline of the Orders, was framed for men of robuster mould and unspeakably less sensitive nerves. Their obstacle was that of opulence; they served God, as they foreswore Him, with wasteful thoroughness. Our obstacle is that of poverty. Onr ancestors put out their follies at compound interest and we are reaping the harvest. The human frame has, Mr. Thompson believes, under this burden and under the complications of modern life suffered a radical diminution of sheer vital power. No faculty has increased except the faculty of suffering, for in the elaboration of its nerves it has become, as it were, soaked in mind. It cries out not for a curb against the excess of its passions, but for the energy to be passionate at all, "Merely to front existence, for some, is a surrender of self, a choice of ineludibly rigorous abnegation." Surely then we must treat our bodies after another fashion than that of old if we are to make them fit receptacles for sanctity? Mr. Thompson thinks so, and he has discovered a wise director of souls, the late Archbishop Porter, S.J., who thought with him. "Better to eat meat on Good Friday," writes the Archbishop, "than to live in war with every one about us. I fear much you do not take enough food and rest. You stand in need of both, and it is not wise to starve yourself into misery." And he prescribes Vichy and Carlsbad against a visitation of evil thoughts. It is an ascesis no less than the other, and no less difficult. We must study to take our bodies with that shrewd and half humorous gravity which we find in nearly all the wise, and to rule by obeying them. "That the demon could have been purged from Saul by medicinal draughts," writes Mr. Thompson in a sentence worthy of Sir Thomas Browne, "were a supposition too much in the manner of the Higher Criticism." But Dryden tells us that whenever "he had a poem to write"—divine tradesman—he choose that method

of depurating his spirit. It is hardly a point to dwell
on. But let us put an end to the old boycott of the
body. Let us be tender and thrifty of its forces. In
the strange commerce of spirit and matter, a holiday,
prudently taken, may be not only better than a
half-done duty, but better even than a wandering
prayer.

Such is the drift of *Health and Holiness*, and no
one who has any appreciation of the grounds on
which it rests will be likely to dispute the conclusion.
As against the practice of certain Orders it may be
a necessary protest; and there is no head of a
convent or college (so long engaged in the great
Intermediate conspiracy) but will profit by reading
it. We laymen must look to ourselves, and the
Church, as we know her, is amply indulgent. She
does not debilitate us with fasts and penances. What
is of far deeper interest than these special applica-
tions of it is the noble philosophy which glimpses
through the book. The temper of Plotinus, who was
so shamed of his body that he always refused to disclose the date or place of his birth, possesses, of
course, a relative truth, but it has been far too dominant within the Church. We have forgotten that
the Scholastics built psychology on the *compositum
humanum*, the dual unit of soul and body. We have
forgotten that the body is the temple of the Holy
Ghost, or remembered it only at catechism time.
But so it is, and in the light of this interpretation
the trivialities of every-day shine with an unsuspected
poetry. It is an interpretation confirmed by all our
fairest instincts. Most of us have had moments when
sensations of which we are commonly a little ashamed
lost their supposed grossness, when a cup of milk
drunk among the mountains had in it a lyric ecstasy,
and the least spiritual of the senses was transfused
with spirit. I do not speak of those experiences
which Coventry Patmore touched with the rapture

of his vision; but in his poem *To the Body* the whole essence of *Health and Holiness* is to be found. As men come back to the simplicities of life their minds grow more habitable tc thoughts like these. The growing nausea of cities, the desire to live in the nearer intimacy of air and earth, the yearning for physical health, of which I have spoken, are all symptoms of a veritable rehabilitation of the body. What could be more appropriate than that a poet should come at this moment to confirm the indispensable truth amid many extravagances, and to Christianise what otherwise tends to the most naïve Paganism?

Mr. Thompson has his vision of the future. "The remedy for modern lassitude of body, for modern weakness of will, is Holiness. . . . Of the potency, magisterial, benevolent, even tyrannous, which goes forth from the spirit on the body, we have but young knowledge. Nevertheless, it is in rapid act of blossoming. Hypnotism, faith-healing, radium—all these, of such seeming multiple divergence, are really concentrating their rays upon a common centre. When that centre is divined, we shall have scientific witness, demonstrated certification, to the commerce between body and spirit, the regality of will over matter. . . . Then will lie open the truth which now we can merely point to by plausibilities, and fortify by instances, the sanctity is medicinal, Holiness a healer. . . . Health, I have well-nigh said, is Holiness. What if Holiness be Health? . . ." Have we not all a forecast of some such perfect marriage of soul and body, in which the two will be no more at war than thought with word? It is vouchsafed to us here and there in a gracious example, some saint whose every action is ordered with a divine courtesy, some lady who seems to live to an ever-sounding, interior music. Perhaps it is a dream of the glorified rather than of the earthly body; but let us hear the poets when they describe it, lest we should not recognize our inheritance when it comes to us.

It is curious to compare Francis Thompson's vision with that of Guyau, most spiritual of evolutionists. "Pleasure, even physical pleasure growing more and more delicate, and mingling with moral ideas, will become more and more esthetic; we see as the ideal term of evolution a race to which every pleasure will be beautiful, every agreeable action artistic, We should then be like those instruments, which are so amply sonorous, that it is impossible to touch them without evoking a sound of musical value; the lightest stimulus would set in vibration the depths of our moral life. . . . Art will no longer stand severed from life; our consciousness will have grown so vast and so delicate as to be ever alert to the harmony of life, and all our pleasures will bear the sacred seal of beauty."

They are alike ideals; but they help in very different ways to keep alive in us that curiosity which is the seed of the future, and to remind us that man, if not in this life perfectible, is capable of endless progress. The superiority of the Catholic poet is that he reinforces the natural will by waters falling an infinite height from the infinite ocean of Spirit. He has two worlds against one. If we place our Fortunate Islands solely within the walls of space and time, they will dissolve into a mocking dream; for there will always be pain that no wisdom can assuage. They must lie on the edge of the horizon with the glimmer of a strange sea about their shores, and their mountain peaks hidden among the clouds.

1905.

REVERIES OF ASSIZE

It is the last day of the Winter Assizes. If you want a metaphor to drape it in, you may call it the punitive clearing-house of Society. The cheques of crime come in, with sinister crinklings and rustlings, to receive the cancelling stamp which announces that in six months or twenty years—or, it may be, three weeks, with a hempen halter at the end—the criminal will have cleared his account with the State. He may then begin anew . . . if he be sufficiently alive. There is no tragic strain in the air as the sentenced prisoners pass out of the dock to lose their freedom, their clothes, their tobacco, and their names for the stated period. They do not, as that young reporter racing over the last page of his flimsy is sure to write, "appear to realize their position." They are only the raw material of tragedy. They have never, like you and me, read Gorky in bad English. They have not participated in the revival of Greek drama; nor even, with the aid of a free pass, studied the free passions of the Stage Society.

So placed, you would, doubtless, gather about you the purple folds of a sorrow so terrible as to swallow up all remembrance of its cause, and I would mimic wicked marquises who went to the tumbrils with a fine phrase and an incomparable gesture. But the enemy of Society now in the dock, in course of receiving seven years, is probably wondering under his yellow and scrubby face how the skilly will taste, and whether they will wash him very hard in jail.

Seven or eight days in an Assize Court help one to understand the anarchist and his attitude towards crime. The theorists of Anarchism propose to sweep

57

away the whole traditional, minute machinery of
penal law, and leave the criminal to the spontaneous
justice of his neighbours. It may be that the
neighbours will lynch a child-beater, and, shrouding
their faces before a supreme anguish, will let a man
who has killed go free. They will take a human,
not a judicial view of things. But be that as it may,
one does feel intensely that these legal forms and
moulds are too narrow, too icily definite, too blank
to psychology to contain the passionate chaos of
life that is poured into them. Think of the colossal
pretensions of this courthouse—this drab granite
building, with the unwashed mud on its pavements,
and the susurrus of crowds that sweat and chatter
about it ! It is a temple to the Problem of Evil. It
is a temple to the Problem of Evidence. It is a
temple to the Mystery of Death. And when you
have uttered these three words you have called up
the whole moral, intellectual, and metaphysical life
of humanity.

If it were not contempt of court you would rise
up and cry out to all these actors—judge, jury,
counsel, prisoner, policeman—that the tragic halo
is about their heads. You would recall them to the
bitter greatness which they seem to have forgotten.
Sad-robed priests—if your vision could be made fact
—would chant prayers around the smoke of conse-
crated censers in the Doric portico of this Temple
of Fear. And the prisoner, sinner and victim at
once, would go to his doom covered with pity as with
sacrificial garlands.

You may be quite certain that none of these things
will happen. There is no provision made for them in
Stephens' *Digest of the Criminal Law*, or in Archbold
on *Evidence*. To imagine them is to welcome the
decadence. But then, as you look up at the bench,
your eye is caught by a veritable, decadent touch—
the judge's flowers. I do not know whether it is

part of the ritual or not, but I have never been at a Criminal Assizes without seeing that incongruous bunch of flowers—this time they are ragged, white chrysanthemums in a vase of blue china—beside the inkpot in which the judicial pen is dipped as it takes notes of the evidence or records the conviction. It reminds one of Baudelaire's *Fleurs du Mal*, Blossoms of Sin.

But, after all, you may expect anything of the judge. He is a wild symbolist. He wears scarlet to manifest the wrath of the law, and ermine for the purity of the law—a spotted purity, to guess from the specimen before us—and a black cap by times for the gloom of death. Probably there is some guarded mystery in the number of curls in his wig of white horse-hair. And the policemen—it is in Ireland, but crime is as cosmopolitan as money!—are admirable studies in silver and jet; especially the district inspectors, with their braided hussar-jackets and the gleam of chains and brooch-buckles upon them. It seems an artistic impertinence that crime should lift its shaggy head against so many perfumed people, dressed out in such splendid raiment. But great as are the virtues of uniform, they do not quite reach to the total extinction of evil.

You had a sense of utter futility as you listened to the steady, infinitesimal drip of evidence. It was like the nagging and pecking patter of thin rain on a hat. It proved everything with absolute conclusiveness except the moral guilt of the prisoner. You have the same sense of the emptiness of criminology as a pale, sensitive face appears above the spikes of the dock. He might be a poet, an Assisi peasant turned saint, but certainly there is no signature of crime in his visage. As a matter of fact, he stabbed a neighbour to death because of a difference of opinion as to the rate of wages in North Carolina.

It seems a poor reason enough. To act like that is to take truth too heavily, and life too lightly. Besides, there are plenty of things to quarrel about at home without going to Carolina, North or South.

How did the prisoner come to do it? You can see that he is as puzzled to answer the question as anybody else. He stands in the dock clasping and unclasping the fingers of that horrible right hand which held the knife. It seems to him a foreign body: it is surely not his? The late Mr. Browning, perhaps, could explain it. After all, if any truth is of any importance, every truth is of infinite importance. And think of the monstrous spectacle before Heaven of this dead man riding easily about the country sowing stories two dollars a week wrong as to the rate of wages in North Carolina! How many destinies he might mis-shape with his eight-and-fourpenny error! Well, he will propagate no more economic blunders. And his slayer will wear the yellow and arrowed jacket for ten years to come. But will that give back the dead disputant to the sunlight or to his wife?

The courthouse is somehow growing too small. Your brain is growing too small. The world itself is too small for these explosive and shattering speculations. The judge is doing his best; everybody is doing his best; even Mr. Gladstone who undertakes in his Borstal repair-shops to patch up a moral personality, as good as new, for all and divers his Majesty's subjects in prison. If the thing is to be done at all it must be done after this fashion.

Certainly, one has no substitute to offer for this Judaeo-Roman-English criminal law, and, perhaps, equally criminal civilization. Still, one is conscious of a vague protest against it all. In crime, in moral evil, the veiled destinies have set mankind a problem too hard to understand, too heavy to endure. For my part, I can only fall back on the serpent and the apple, and an obscure something which, as my Penny Catechism says, "darkened our understanding, weakened our will, and left in us a strong inclination to evil."

1909.

A NEW WAY
OF MISUNDERSTANDING
HAMLET

What one felt most painfully at Mr. Harvey's recent performance of Hamlet was the artistic bankruptcy of the play. Of course no decent citizen confessed his boredom, because Shakespeare is the keystone of the conventions, a "national asset" as is said in England. But if art means freshness, words with raw, vivid sensation behind them, surprise and an element of strangeness? And what else does it mean? Already a hundred years ago the humane Charles Lamb was able to write that all the shining things in the play had been "so handled and pawed by declamatory boys and men" that for him they were "perfect dead members." And since then! The great Law of Ennui has vindicated itself even against Shakespeare. He has been mummified into an orthodoxy. He is a field for antiquarians, a proud heritage, an excuse for sumptuous scenery, but as an artist in the strict sense he hardly exists. Only one thing can restore him, a prolonged bath of oblivion. If he is to be brought to life again he must be redeemed from his immortality, which will be better than to redeem his house from the Americans. Societies must be started to destroy his works, at all events to lose them for a hundred and fifty years, and so make it possible for unborn happier generations to come to him as to a fresh and breathing phenomenon. Failing that he must be excluded from all school and university courses, and forbidden under heavy penalties to any one not having attained his majority.

The pity is that, with the calamity of so long life, he should not have the happiness to be understood. The inky Dane, in especial, has had as evil fortune in this regard as if he had walked the actual earth and devoted himself to politics. Critic after critic has arisen to misrepresent him, and this secular misrepresentation has so crept into the empire of our imagination that direct vision of the play is impossible. Tieck's Hamlet we know, and Goethe's and Coleridge's and Mr. Tree's and Mr. Harvey's, but Shakespeare's Hamlet no man knows. Shakespeare's Hamlet, as a painful matter of fact, no man can ever know. We know how much sub-meaning and personal colour the same set of words takes on in different minds, and that these are never exactly what they were in the creator's mind. And then in Hamlet there is the added barrier of Elizabethan English, and the fact that Shakespeare is as topical as a pantomime. What each of us does is to construct a private understanding of Hamlet (which is certain to be a misunderstanding) out of materials furnished conjointly by ourselves, Shakespeare, a cloud of critics, and the actor who happens to be concrete before our eyes at the moment ; and it is in confession of this, and not as a poor paradox, that the title of this paper has been devised.

The points I wish modestly to put forward here will be most intelligible as a comment on the popular reading. That reading has one merit at least, that of simplicity. According to it the plastic principle of the play, or rather the flaw that suffers it to stream down its ruinous course, is a vice of character— Hamlet's "inability to act." It is Goethe's "oak planted in a costly vase which should have only borne pleasant flowers " ; it is Coleridge's "man living in meditation, called upon to act by every motive, human and divine, but the great object of whose

life is defeated by continually resolving to do, yet
doing nothing but resolve." These are the phrases
that have captured the general mind, and flowed
like a mist over the outlines of the play. But
consider for a moment. Remembering Goethe's
paltry performance—thanks to his superculture—
in the liberation of Germany, and the lamentable
life story of Coleridge, who can doubt that we have
here not so much the poet's imagination as that of
his critics? *Quicquid recipitur secundum modum reci-
pientis*, we get out of things what we bring to them ;
and I submit that the apocalypse of moral insuffi-
ciency discerned by these two eminent minds in
Hamlet was brought with them in the satchels of
their conscience. They are simply making General
Confessions at the expense of the unfortunate Prince.
Let us analyse this interpretation popularized by
them. The kernel of it is this. It demands in the
place of Hamlet a crude, gory, gullible, instantanous
savage who not only believes in ghosts but lacks
even the elementary savage's knowledge that there
are evil as well as good ghosts, and whose will is
hung on a hair-trigger dischargeable by the airiest
impulse and subject to no restraint, moral or pru-
dential. The commercial blandness with which
people talk of Hamlet's " plain duty " makes one
wonder if they recognize such a thing as plain
morality. The "removal," of an uncle without
due process of law and on the unsupported statement of an unsubpœnable ghost ; the widowing of
a mother and her casting-off as unspeakably vile,
are treated as enterprises about which a man has no
right to hesitate or even to feel unhappy. Because,
meshed about with murder, adultery, usurpation,
espionage, hypocrisy, and all other natural horrors,
reinforced by the still greater horror of the super-
natural, because in these cheerful conditions Hamlet
is healthy-minded enough to grow "thought-sick,"

he is marked down as one "unstable as water."
What bewilders most of all is that there lurks in
the popular view (and I appeal to the general experience) a vague conviction that if Hamlet had only
shown himself morally-fibrous enough, all the blood
and tears would somehow have been averted and
the curtain would fall on a serene Denmark.

I do not deny that a tragedy derived from superculture and a feeble will would be admirable.
Indeed if it be wanted it can be found in the purest
essence in Turgéneff's *Rudin*. But I submit that
this is not the true ethos of *Hamlet*. I submit that
Hamlet, so far from being the most "internal" of
Shakespeare's plays, is nearly the most "external,"
and has for plastic principle not character but that
veiled force which we call destiny. What, in fine,
is it but a tale of justice, bloodily executed
through what seem "accidental judgments, casual
slaughters"? Such indeed was the reading of the
Prince himself:—

> Heaven hath pleased it so
> To punish me with this, and this with me,
> That I must be their scourge and minister.

The problem is set wholly from the outside. It is
not a product of Hamlet's superculture, but of the
sin of his uncle and the lesser sin of his mother,
and it is a problem so overwhelming that, however
it be handled and by whatever type of character, it
must issue in abundant tears and blood. What is
claimed here for Hamlet's solution is, that it is the
only one justified by the character of the evidence
and the practical means at his command, and that,
above all, it is justified by results. The destinies
approve and aid him, and when the curtain falls on
a terrible harvest of horror we feel, nevertheless, a
deep appeasement. The agony of Hamlet is over,
the due ransom of sin has been paid with lives guilty

and innocent, and with the inearthing of much moral
refuse, the world sweeps into pure air again. The
roll of Fortinbras' drums is not so much the irony
as the recuperative force of life, lingering with praise
over the body of him who has made recuperation
possible.

This is a point which must not be ignored : the
play ends, thanks to Hamlet's course of action, in
absolutely the best way in which it could end. The
king, of course, was due to the sword. But surely
Gertrude also is better out of the world than in it ?
Had she lived there was nothing but the gnawing of
the worm, shame and remorse, or perhaps—and the
closet scene shows her capable of it—the triumph of
the fouler part of her, and the pursuit of her son
with hatred and vengeance. Does anybody drop
tears over Laertes, that polished cutter of throats i'
the church ? There remain Polonius and Ophelia.
The comic side of Polonius is always played with
such over-emphasis as to hide the dangerous side of
him. His complicity in the murder of the elder
Hamlet may be disputed, although it is not easy
otherwise to explain his overweening influence with
Claudius. He certainly conspired with the latter in
his usurpation, and we cannot say what is the bound
to his falseness. Suppose he had not been slain
behind the arras, but had lived to carry his tale to
Claudius, what course of action would he have coun-
selled ? Like son, like father; his plan would have
differed from the poisoned rapier only in being,
perhaps, a little more politic. Polonius helps to
remind us that we may have comic murderers, just
as the Burghleys and other contemporary statesmen
show that we may have pious murderers. As for
Ophelia, she is one of those who are organized for
unhappiness. Hamlet's disgust with life is so violent,
just and incurable that the old magic of their love
can never return, and his straits are such that, how-

ever he acts, enough misery will be produced to dethrone her frail reason.

I have submitted also that the evidence in Hamlet's possession never reaches that daylight certainty which justifies private vengeance. If Shakespeare had intended to exhibit a mind which is at once absolutely sure of itself and incapable of action, would he not have brought the murder to light by the agency of some courtier who had secretly witnessed it? In fact the ghost is the one great blot and uncombining ingredient in the play. Had Shakespeare preserved the mental climate of the original story the ghost might perhaps have been tolerated, but he is quite out of joint with so thorough a modern as Hamlet. He complicates the whole action, and steeps it in incongruity. Hamlet's desire to have more relative grounds than the word of this visitant in whom it is impossible to believe fully except during his actual presence is in the highest degree natural. He therefore tries the experiment of the play, and fails. What he had hoped was to provoke Claudius to "proclaim his malefaction" in the ear of the court, for the case that has to be built up is one that will convince not only Hamlet, but also the public at large. What really is provoked? A temporary indisposition which can be explained away in two sentences the next day. It may convince Hamlet, but it certainly would not secure his acquittal before a jury.

But even supposing him to be justifiably certain, has he the practical means to kill Claudius without, by the same act, surrendering himself to death? Claudius was popular enough to override Hamlet's claims and have himself chosen king. In that office he had shown competence, his relations with England and Norway being most excellent. He had a levy of three thousand men in the immediate neighbourhood of the court whom he kept in good humour by

frequent carousals. His courtiers were so loyal that
the Court-play apparently awoke not the least
suspicion or hostility in a single one of them, and
that, even after Laertes' confession of his treachery,
when Hamlet plunges his rapier into Claudius, they
shriek "Treason! Treason!" and would no doubt
have cut the young prince down were that not plainly
superfluous. As against this, Hamlet is a student,
just come home, super-intelligent and a hater of bores
and shams. His opinion of the masquerade of royalty
may be gathered from that one remark of his: "Let's
to the Court! for, by my fay, I cannot reason." He
applies his literary criticism to every-day conversation, and analyses received platitudes with the most
ruthless candour. To crown all, he is a Temperance
Pioneer! In short, the situation is such that no one
would have much chance of organizing support
enough to oust Claudius, but that Hamlet, by the
sheer force of his superiorities, has no chance at all.
Of course it is always possible for him to slay the
king and sacrifice his own life to his vengeance. But
that would be something worse even than "hire and
salary," and he has no enthusiasm for dying. Many
people assume that he has, but in fact he is philosopher enough to be afraid of death. True, like every
man of high intellect, he has moments of moral
nausea, when he almost thinks that the best thing
is not to be born, the next best to leave life as quickly
as may be. But he recoils from the invisible event;
above all, he never caresses the idea of suicide. The
great "to be or not to be" monologue, sometimes
interpreted in this sense, is really the precise opposite.
It is rather an admonition to himself to defy death
which he sees to be probably bound up with his
revenge, and not to suffer his great enterprise, to be
turned away by the fear of death. In short he never
is absolutely certain of the facts of the crime, nor in
a position to punish it with safety to himself. And,

although Shakespeare cannot amend this latter circumstance, he does amend the former, and with exquisite dramatic courtesy allows Hamlet full evidence of the king's guilt of another murder before calling his retributive sword into action.

What counts against Hamlet in popular estimation is his continual self-reproach. But this springs just from his exacting ideal of action, for he would shorten a straight line to reach his end. Religious biography will furnish a parallel; it is not among the actual sinners that we find self-contempt and a consciousness of the unforgiveable sin, but among the Bunyans and the Saint Alphonsus Ligouris. There is another motive behind Hamlet's outbursts. He is not certain enough to act, but his tense and tortured mind must find relief, and words are not irrevocable. But after the emotional debauch of his monologues, the lucid judgment returns, with its questionings and firm grasp of difficulties. Hamlet is compromised also by the speculative embroideries which his mind works over the drab stuff of experience. People think with Horatio that it is "to enquire too curiously" to find the dust of Alexander stopping a beer-barrel. But is it? Is not Hamlet rather the avid intellect, which must needs think out of things everything that is to be found in them? "Hamlet's obstacles are internal." He certainly has internal obstacles. He is hampered by conscience, natural affection, an exquisite taste and a capacity for metaphysics; very grave obstacles, if what is desired is immediate bloodshed. Some critics hold that Shakespeare wrote *Hamlet* to purge his countrymen of these qualities which he perceived spreading, to the infinite prejudice of Elizabethan Jingoism. It may be so, and I am free to confess that, as far as public policy goes, his countrymen have reformed them indifferently. But it is just because of these failings that Hamlet possesses human significance. Without them, he might be very interesting from the point of view of a tiger, but

he would never have touched and troubled our
imagination. As it is, we think of him as the noble
and courtly prince who passes through life, annotating
it with a gloss of melancholy speculation that has
been absorbed into the mind of Europe, and who so
confronts it practically that the destinies adopt him
for their minister, and, through him, draw out of
unexampled horrors, justice and even a certain
terrible peace.[1]

As a perhaps tedious supplement, I submit that
the character of Horatio has been as favourably, as
that of Hamlet has been unfavourably, misunderstood.
He enjoys the reputation of being the strong, silent,
truly virile man, held up in contrast to the gusty and
barren metaphysician. In support of this there can
be produced just a single speech of Hamlet's: against
it there is the whole of Horatio's words and actions.
The eulogy, like so many other passages, has, however,
never been construed in its dramatic context. It is
spoken, be it remembered, immediately before the
play, when Hamlet is tense with the most terrible
expectation. He is about to probe the King's
conscience to the quick, and naturally wants cor-
roboration of his own prejudiced eyes, and perhaps
assistance in the scene that may follow. In order to
induce the deplorable Horatio to render even this
petty service it is necessary to flatter him, and the
exaggerated courtesy, natural to Hamlet—as in the
reception of Rosencranz and Guildenstern—combines
with his immediate need to produce superlatives.
His own fine taste rebels against them, and, as is

---

[1] The only sustainable charge that can be made against Hamlet
is one of over-hasty action—with regard, I mean, to Rosencranz
and Guildenstern. He sent them to death without anything like
decisive proof of their complicity in the design to have him
executed in England. There is nothing to show that they knew
the contents of the original commission ; indeed the contrary is
established by their continuing their journey after losing Hamlet.
Most people will, however, accept the latter's justification o
himself as satisfactory.

known, he concludes with "something too much of
this!" (Were I a German I would suggest that
these words are an amending note of Shakespeare on
the MS., which he is known to have been revising,
that he meant to recast the lines, and that his private
note has been interpolated into Hamlet's speech.)
What, as a matter of fact, is Horatio's record in
the play? He is at Elsinore two months before
he thinks it worth while to call on his old friend
Hamlet, although he knows the latter to be in the
most grievous trouble. At the first appearance of
the ghost he has not wit enough to address it in
Latin, although that is what he was brought there
for by Marcellus. At the second appearance he is
not able even to tell Hamlet the time, and later is
guilty of a much grosser ineptitude. Marcellus
urges him to come on after the Prince and the
ghost. "Oh!" says Horatio, "Heaven will direct
it!" and his delegation of his duty to Providence
has to be crushed by Marcellus' "Nay, let's follow
him." At what stage he comes to know of the
King's crime is not clear, but he certainly possesses
all Hamlet's knowledge of it after the the Court
Play. And what does this strong silent man do?
Organize a party, as Laertes found friends to
oraganize one, to execute vengeance against
Cladius? By no means. He has nothing better
to say than that he very well noted the King and
that Hamlet ought to rhyme the quatrain in which
his frenzy extravagates. Afterwards, when the
Prince is sent to England under the most sinister
circumstances, does the good Horatio make an
attempt either to accompany or to liberate him?
As a matter of fact he lies conscientiously low, and
cultivates the best relations with Cladius. His next
opportunity is at Hamlet's relation of his escape
from the death intended for him in England.
Horatio has indeed the grace to admire Hamlet's
superior firmness of character—"Why, what a king

is this!"—but he does his best to cancel this by sympathetic tears over Rosencranz and Guildenstern. Before the duel he administers draughts of discouragement and superstition, and he has not the sense to see that Laertes' rapier is unbated. In fact from beginning to end he is a wandering ineptitude who has never a single suggestion, and whose speech consists mainly of " Ay, my Lords," " That is most certain," " Is it possible," and other helpful phrases. At the last he has one good impulse to finish the poisoned cup, but the dying Hamlet intervenes, and Horatio addresses himself to funeral orations which are certainly much more after his heart. He is prayed merely to absent himself from felicity awhile, but we may be sure that he does not construe the last as the emphatic word, but stands in as an echo to Fortinbras and absents himself as long as possible. And this is the strong silent man after whom Hamlet should have modelled himself! In truth he compares poorly with Osric, who was at any rate a stylist.

I cannot abstain from a word on Hamlet as an art critic. His theory that the stage should hold the mirror up to nature is of course absurd, at least as far as gesture and outer expression of emotion goes. I refer rather to his employment of art as an oblique moral inquisition—a most remarkable anticipation of what Browning has to say in the Epilogue of " The Ring and the Book"; and to his delightful prophetic criticism of the two great achievements of the modern theatre—the musical comedy and the problem play. Polonius has grown impatient at the length of the fine epic passage recited by the players; Hamlet turns on him with his unforgettable "Oh, he must have a jig or a tale of bawdy, or he falls asleep."

1905.

YOUNG EGYPT

GENEVA, *September* 1909.

The Congress of the Jeunesse Egyptienne is over. The Rue Bartholomy is no longer splashed with the crimson and scarlet of the tarbouch which one learns is the correct term for what we more naturally call the fez. And as one sits by the lake shore, drowsed with the dim and misted beauty of the Swiss September, there are no grave, dark faces, no star and crescent favours, no cataracts of vowelled Arabic to force one back again to the dusty duties of political conflict.

All this is to say that the Congress, as a spectacle, was brilliant and picturesque. The Jeunesse Egyptienne is, to a large extent, a jeunesse dorée. It is also a movement of intellectuals. The great body of the delegates were students—students in law, medicine, or arts—who thronged here from Lyons, Paris, Dijon, Oxford. The President, M. Mohamed Fahmy, is a " free professor " of Mahometan law at the University of Geneva. Hamed El Alaily, who read perhaps the most brilliant paper at the Congress, " A Plea for a Constructive Policy," is at Oxford, and carries about him a curious sense at once of the fine essence of Oxford and the fine essence of that Arab culture which gave us Avicenna and Averroës. M. Loutfi Goumah, who swept the Congress off its feet on the second day with a passionate reply to Mr. Keir Hardie, entertains me in the evening with a lecture on Eastern lyrical poetry. When Egypt is free he assures me with a smile that he will at last have time to complete a

73

criticism of German philosophy from the Arabic point of view.

Decidedly whatever you may call the Young Egyptians, you cannot call them uneducated or irresponsible. On the contrary, they manifest every sign of wealth, culture, knowledge of the world, and a courtesy suave beyond expression. There is a wide range of racial types from the noble Arabian profile to something that seems almost Ethiopian. In social intercourse one is impressed by the fact that they have all gone to a good tradition for their manners and to a good tailor for their clothes. One is impressed still more by the evidences of firmness of character. Hardly any of them touches wine. Most of them do not seem to smoke. " You see," says one of the non-smokers, " tobacco darkens the complexion. And, mon Dieu! am I not dark enough already ? "

Whether this abstinence has any religious sanction at the present day is a matter difficult to determine. One hardly thinks so; and yet I have a picture of a stout and amiable pasha at the Congress slipping his Rosary Beads through his fingers with incredible industry, with a murmur for each bead of " Allah !"

For the moment there is one binding idea, and only one, dominent in the assembly, and that is not a religious but a political idea. Three parties are represented, grading down from fierce extremists to somewhat timid reformers, but let a speaker fling out the cry of " Egypt for the Egyptians," and Conservative hands clap as loudly as Radical hands to a fusillade of " Très biens " and " Bravos." The Congress is inspired by a sincere passion for nationality. It has no hatred for England except in so far as Egypt cannot belong at the same time to the English and to the Egyptians.

And here I must signalize the dramatic moment of the proceedings. Just as every picture has its centre of repose, so every assembly has its centre of tension. At Geneva this central point was found when M. Loutfi Goumah leaped to his feet to reply to some things that Mr. Keir Hardie had said, and to other things which he had not said. " Mr. Hardie has spoken of helping us to achieve ' some effective form of self-government.' We do not want ' some effective form of self-government.' Egypt demands a free constitution, flowing to her not from the British Parliament but from her own monarch, the Khedive. Mr. Hardie promises to ask questions in tho House of Commons. What sort of questions? He will ask whether Cairo has a good drainage system, and whether the water is drinkable in Alexandria. But we want fundamental questions about fundamental matters. We want him to ask what is to be the date of the evacuation."

My duty is not to appraise, but merely to chronicle facts, and without discussing the strange interpretation which exhibited Mr. Hardie as a Conservative, I have only to say that as M. Goumah proceeded with his speech, the tides of passion rose higher and higher in the Congress, and that he resumed his chair amid a tumult of cheers. Crimson tarbouches bobbed their way to the platform, and groups of students flung themselves on the orator, embracing him, and kissing his hands. " The Mazzini of Egypt!" shouted somebody beside me in the crowd.

Undoubtedly he is one of the men of the future. Small and spare, with a drooping moustache, he throbs with such intense energy that you expect to see electric sparks leap out of his gesturing figure. He speaks French, English, and Arabic with the same fluent precision. He has the gift of epigram, and, unlike his compatriots, a quick sense of humour. With Hamed El Alaily, and Mohamed Fahmy—this latter a striking figure with countless centuries of Oriental shrewdness in his face—he constitutes the pivot around which this new movement will revolve.

Opinions differ, and hopes will be disappointed, but for my part I regard this second Congress as opening a new epoeh in the Egyptian Nationalist movement. The actual work of the three days, including the foundation of a new propagandist journal and the initiation of a system of free national schools in Egypt, has already been recorded in the newspapers. I am concerned only to give some faint sense of the tone and atmosphere of the Congress. It was alive in every fibre. The papers read, although somewhat too encyclopædic for the occasion, were the work of cultured men. The few differences as to details merely lent relief to the keenness and enthusiasm of the assembly. And with all this there was behind the whole programme a sincere desire for peace. The so-called "violence" of the speeches consisted merely in saying what every Englishman has heartily said with Simon De Montfort, and Hampden, and Locke, and John Stuart Mill.

.   .   .   .

Much has happened since the Geneva Congress. That Tartuffe-Tartarin, Colonel Roosevelt, has trailed the Stars and Stripes in the foulest mud of Imperialism. M. Briand has forbidden the Congress of 1910 to meet in Paris, and, thereby, proclaimed the nothingness of France in international politics. The Suez Canal affair has on the one hand, unified national feeling in Egypt, and, on the other, has provoked British Imperialists to a fresh campaign in favour of annexation. The problem has grown more acute, and at the same time more soluble. The Canal is the difficulty. But if the Canal be definitely neutralized, on terms fair to Egypt and England alike, what pretext will then remain for the maintenance of the occupation?

THE FATIGUE
OF ANATOLE FRANCE[1]

[1] *L'Ile des Pingouins. Les Contes de Jacques Tournebroche.* By Anatole France. 1908.

The autumn of M. Anatole France is coloured by the one vanity of human existence against which his soul had not hitherto adventured: he has become popular. "My last years," Schopenhauer used to say, "bring me roses, but they are white roses." It may be that there is a like pallor in the coronals which have of late been showered so abundantly on the great French master of irony, tenderness, and despair. It may be that he experiences but a sombre consolation at seeing his radiant and incomparable prose rendered, with many refractions into English. But at all events he has achieved notoriety. Certain of his phrases—poison in crystal cups or ambrosia of the gods in vinegar-vials: who shall say?—have been finally adopted into the gold currency of literature. The man himself is no longer a veiled prophet. The famous bust in which he looks out over an Hebraic nose between a stiff imperial and what seems to be a loose forage cap, has passed through Europe, at least in photogravure. The book-reader of Brixton has been impelled as urgently as the bookseller of his own Quai Malaquais to guess at the secret behind that ridged and ambiguous mask. The face, some of his interpreters have said, is that of a *Bénédictin narquois*. Rather is it the face of a soldier ready to die for a flag in which he does not entirely believe, on condition, be it understood, that he shall not be asked to die in a tragic or, as one might say, in a

77

muddy fashion. He looks out at you like a veteran
of the lost cause of intellect, to whose soul the trumpet
of defeat strikes with as mournful and vehement a
music as to that of Pascal himself, but who thinks
that a wise man may be permitted to hearten himself
up in evil days with an anecdote after the manner
of his master Rabelais.

M. France has achieved notoriety, but hardly
happiness. If *L'Ile des Pingouins* has been one of
the best discussed volumes of late years, it is none
the less a bulletin of fatigue, which notifies us of the
burial of yet another illusion. The book, indeed,
seems intended as the last chapter of a period. In it
Anatole France, savant, stylist, and Olympian, pronounces with affection and contempt a funeral
discourse over Anatole France, republican, Socialist,
and Dreyfusard. The man of letters lays aside, with
smiling sadness, the sword of a fighting publicist, and
an interesting case of dual personality comes to an
end. The Socialists are naturally in despair, At
least one critic, belonging to that party, confesses
that he has long entertained doubts not merely about
the stability of M. France, but even about his sales,
and thinks it probable that an edition of one of his
books nowadays means only two hundred copies.
But had not his greatest interpreter, George Brandes,
foreseen the present reversion to type, as one may
call it? "It may be," wrote Brandes, after hearing
the master speak at a Socialist meeting in the Paris
Trocadero in 1904, "that as tbe popular orator—a
career for which he was not intended by nature—
he has proclaimed himself rather more strongly
convinced than he is in his inmost soul." Had not
Doctor Trublet in *L'Histoire Comique* separated
himself for ever from the "advanced" thinkers who
believe that republicanism is the final truth of politics,
and that by the application of this truth the human
race is infinitely perfectible? "My business," says

Trublet, "is to comfort men and console" them.
How can one comfort or console anybody without
lying? It was not that M. France refused to make
sacrifices to the will to believe in political Utopias.
On the contrary, he went so far as to write an
introduction to the collected speeches of M. Emile
Combes. and even, it was said, to read the novels of
M. Zola. Having thus acquired a firm faith in
humanity, he was at pains to record it in the course
of a speech on Renan. "Lentement, mais toujours,
l'humanité réalise les rêves des sages." That was in
1903. In 1908, having come to understand that the
process of realization is as slow as the movement of
a glacier and as tortuous as the way of an eagle in
the air, he returns to the orbit of his temperament.
His futility on Blessed Jeanne d'Arc laid aside, he
contributes an introduction to the memoirs of
Mademoiselle Loie Fuller, a dancer, aud publishes
Penguin Island and *Les Contes de Jacques Tournebroche*.

L'Ile des Pingouins is to all intents a comic history
of France. The narrative is introduced by a characteristic preface, in which the author of so many
brilliant reconstructions of the past denies, and not
for the first time, the possibility of any history,
serious or comic. He consults the masters of
paleography, but they indignantly decline to be
called historians.. Who has ever detected them in
an attempt to distil the scantiest trickle of life or
truth from a document? That is an enterprise which
may attract vain and imaginative persons, but for
their part they work in the spirit of positive science.
They confine themselves to verifiable facts—that is
to say, to texts—and refuse to be tempted into the
fantastic world of ideas. It is possible to be certain
about the shape of words, but not about their
significance. M. France passes on to the recognized
historians, who are shocked to find that he proposes
to write an original history. An original historian,

they assure him, is the object of universal distrust and contempt. History may very well be the lie agreed upon ; the great point is that it is agreed upon. Readers of history do not like to be surprised; they look to find only the stupidities with which they are already familiar, and regard any novel suggestion as an affront to some cherished belief. The historian must therefore be on his guard against originality. He must also be respectful towards established institutions, and, on these two conditions, success is within his grasp. Fortified by these counsels M. France proceeds, in much humility of spirit, to narrate the story of the island of Alca, from its beginnings in hagiography to its ending in dynamite. There is little need to set out here in any detail the substance of the book. The title is easily explained. The old saint Maël, a missionary of deep faith but defective eyesight, is transported to the Arctic regions in a miraculous stone trough. There, mistaking a colony of penguins for men and philosophers, he pronounces the formula of baptism over them, and creates a theological *impasse* which can only be relieved by the actual transformation of the penguins into human shape. The island is then towed by Saint Maël to the coast of Brittany, and there under the name of Penguinia, or Alca, it enters the comity of civilization. It evolves through the customary stages, inventing in turns clothes— a suggestion of the devil—individual property, a royal dynasty, a patron saint, and the taxation of the weak for the benefit of the strong. These matters afford obvious scope for the subtle and perverse spirit of M. France. The pages on the origin of property are not only powerful but even passionate : his heart is for the moment engaged in the writing. A chapter on the mediæval art of Penguinia gives him an opportunity to parody, with delightful malice, the English theorists of the pre-Raphaelite movement. But it must be confessed that the first half of the book languishes on the perilous edge of dullness. The serene improprieties with which M. France annotates his Lives of the Saints, mingling, as one might say, the odour of the smoke-room with the odour of sanctity, are very Latin, but not very amusing. M. France himself seems to perceive that his grasp on his material is weakening: he makes an abrupt plunge from the Renaissance into modern history, and his sprightliness is at once restored. The second part, comprising more than half the entire volume, is a continuation and conclusion of the novels which have been published since 1897 under the general title of *Histoire Contemporaine.* The cometary career of Boulanger and the Dreyfus Affaire are reconstructed with incomparable verve. Every phrase tells, every figure moves in the glow of supreme comedy. The Visire Ministry, which was carried into office by the reaction in favour of Dreyfus, " declared itself prudently progressive. Paul Visire and his colleagues were eager for reforms, and it was only in order to avoid compromising the prospect of these reforms that they refrained from proposing them. For they were deep politicians, and they knew that to propose a reform is to compromise it." From history we pass on to prophecy. The fate of the Clemenceau Ministry, plunged ultimately by rich Jews, reckless journalists, and the intrigues of one Madame Cérès ieto an irreparable war, is somewhat vaguely outlined; and in a last chapter we are permitted to see M. France's vision of the future. It is not a very cheerful vision. The continued concentration of industry has evolved a society of but two classes, millionaires and employees. The millionaire type exhibits the physical characteristics of Mr. Rockefeller developed to the last limit of possibility. Drier of body, thinner of lip, and yellower of complexion than the old Spanish monks, they cultivate a mysticism and even an asceticism of opulence. Living in their offices on eggs and milk, they have no intercourse with the world save through the medium of an electric button : they steadily amass wealth of which they no longer see even the metallic symbols, and acquire infinite means for the satisfaction of desires which they no longer experience. The material constituents of this world of the future are monstrous and tentacular cities, temples of " slaughterous industry, infamous specu- lations, hideous luxury, and a colossal uniformity of ugliness." Such a society cannot be reformed; it can only be destroyed. And under the shattering logic of dynamite, or rather of an explosive to which dynamite is as the crackle of a schoolboy's squib, the world of clerks and capitalists dissolves. An entire civilization is effaced, and wild horses pasture on the site of the capital of Alca. Then the story of civilization begins anew, the story without an end. The hunter comes, and after him, in a dreary cycle, the shepherd, the tiller of the soil, the weaver of wool, the worker in iron. The effaced civilization is, with infinite labour rebuilt. Once more we are in a world of millionaires and employees, of monstrous and tentacular cities. . . . The thing that has been is the thing that shall be, and the achievement of the future will be as that of the past. The epitaph of generations unborn will be that which has been written upon the tombstones of generations forgotten. " They were born, they suffered, they died." It is the Eternal Return of ancient philosophy, in a garment more sombre than any of which the ancients ever dreamed. It is less an Eternal Return, than an eternal and infinitely monotonous tautology.

Such is the wisdom to which Anatole France has come, after wandering for ten years in the desert of politics. One recalls the circumstances under which he came to appear in the *rôle* of a publicist. The year 1897 witnessed his election to the Immortals ; it also witnessed the publication of the first two volumes of his *Histoire Contemporaine*. Until that year he had not descended from his tower of ivory to discover the actual world. In his candidature for the Academy he was regarded as a Conservative, and was opposed to Ferdinand Fabre, a writer notorious for his hostility to the Church. There is no need to suggest a corrupt silence on his part, or a sinister coincidence ; but the truth is that once safely installed in the chair vacated by M. Ferdinand de Lesseps, he began to exhibit an active interest in politics. He put his head out of the window, discovered the Dreyfus Affaire, and took his stand with the Socialists. He revised his judgments, even in matters of literature. Zola, whose "disgusting celebrity" he had declined to envy, and of whom he had written that no man had "so exerted himself to abase humanity, and to deny everything that is good and right," became for him not only a valiant citizen, but even a great novelist, "whose harping had raised up a spacious city of the ideal." In the interval M. France has had a wider experience of politics ; he has rubbed intimate shoulders with the prophets of progress, and has watched the flux of events and the transformations of men. It would be unjust to say that *Penguin Island* is a recantation of his democratic and socialistic utterances. He is still the son of the Revolution, and there is a tremor of sincere passion in his voice as he tells us of the grimed and hungry workers who swarm out in times of Royalist aggression to defend the Republic—the Republic which nevertheless is to them a symbol of hope merely and not of fulfilment. He proclaims not the bankruptcy of Socialism, but rather the emptiness of politics as

such. It is impossible not to identify France with
his own Bidault-Coquille, the student of asteroids.
Bidault-Coquille had come down from the old fire-
escape, from which he was accustomed to observe
the heavens, in order to fight for the eternal
principles of justice which he took to be involved
in the Affaire Pyrot or Dreyfus. He found himself
in alliance with hysterical adventuresses, ambitious
generals, vain journalists, and the St. Pauls of
Socialism, eager for Utopia, but also eager for
portfolios. Justice is triumphant, but the triumph
is clouded with meanness, and he returns to his
asteroids, disillusioned, and disillusioned most of
all with regard to his own motives. " Go back to
your fire-escape and your stars," he says to himself,
" but go back in humility of spirit. You thought
to yourself, ' I will step down into the streets and
show myself a noble and valiant citizen. Then I
shall be able to repose calmly in the esteem of my
contemporaries and the approval of history.' But
you have not even suffered for conscience sake ; for
with the decay of belief and character your countrymen have become incapable of that savagery which
once lent a tragic greatness to the conflict of ideas.
Now that you have buried your illusions ; now that
you know how hard it is to redress injustice and
how one must be ever beginning anew, you are going
back to your asteroids. Go back then ! but go back
in humility of spirit."

The conclusion was inevitable, and rightly considered it casts no sort of discredit upon politics. It
is no doubt useful that parliament-men should be
credulous of their power to create by Statute a new
heaven and a new earth. It is perhaps excusable
that Socialism should believe in the infinite perfectability of the human race. But it is necessary
that the world of culture should retain its sense of
limitation. Humanity must at all costs refuse to be

satisfied with itself. If progress belongs at all to the sphere of real things and of good things, its future depends on those who rise up to question its reality. Faust cannot be redeemed except by the serviceable hostility of Mephistophles. Anatole France is a scandal and a stumbling-block to many serious minds. Of the deep waters of religion he has never tasted; he is a sense short, or, as the psychologists say, he has a blind spot on his soul. But that much said, is it not wise to remember that Ecclesiastes also is among the prophets? Is not the whole Christian conception of life rooted in pessimism, as becomes a philosophy expressive of a world in which the ideal can never quite overcome the crumbling incoherence of matter? May we not say of all good causes what Arnold said only of the proud and defeated Celts: "They went down to battle but they always fell?" Behind politics there is economics; behind economics there is philosophy; and when it comes to a philosophy of values, optimism, with regard to our present plane of experience, can only be regarded as an attractive form of mental disease.

A comparison of *L'Ile des Pingouins* with *Gulliver's Travels* is obvious, although not, perhaps, very illuminating. M. France is suave where Swift is barbaric; he is dainty where Swift is foul; but it is none the less true that Swift's disbelief in humanity was childlike and elementary compared with that which hints itself through *Penguin Island*. Between the two there is the tropical forest of Romanticism with its splendid and noxious blooms: there is the unplumbed, salt, estranging sea of all who have praised death rather than life, from Leopardi and Schopenhauer to D'Annunzio and Hardy. What then? "The life of a people," writes one of the mythical sages quoted in this book, "is a succession of misfortunes, crimes, and stupidities. This is true of the Penguin

nation as of all others. But with that reserve made,
their history is admirable from beginning to end."
There is a certain malice in the phrasing, but who
that has lived and suffered would challenge its
substance of truth? Reason and justice constitute,
no doubt, the elements of a pure science, but it is a
science of very imperfect application to the concrete
world. M, France has had the courage of his discouragement. He has but repeated in terms of
politics what he had already said in terms of art and
erudition, of passion and philosophy—namely, that
the eye is not filled with seeing nor the ear with
hearing. Even more than Bourget, and precisely
because his touch is lighter than Bourget's, and
because he imagines that his rapier is that of an
enemy, he continues the tradition of that Latin and
Catholic pessimism which is so indispensable a
propædeutic to any valorous religion. We have
heard of a tyranny which was tempered by *chansons*.
A pessimism, stabbed and gashed with the radiance
of epigrams, as a thundercloud is stabbed by lightning,
is a type of spiritual life far from contemptible. A
reasonable sadness, chastened by the music of
consummate prose, is an attitude and an achievement
that will help many men to bear with more resignation
the burden of our century. If there be inexcusable
flippancies, and there are many in *L'Ile des Pingouins*,
they belong, perhaps, for the most part to that
temperamental heritage of Latinism which we bar-
barians have never been able to understand. For the
rest, the book is merely an indication that the cobbler
is about to return to his last. After ten years of
politics Anatole France is fatigued, but by expressing
he has banished his fatigue. Two lines of development seem now to be open to him, and, unhappily,
one of them is that *facilis decensus* which his master
Renan chose in his old age. *Les Contes de Jacques
Tournebroche*—a volume with curious red and gold

and blue and gold illustrations by Léon Lébègue—
seems to indicate a declension towards the lower
level of his temperament. It is enough to say of this
collection of stories that it is by turns graceful,
mediocre, and abject, and that there is not a
characteristic turn of phrase or a memorable idea in
it from beginning to end. The other mood in which
M. France may elect to cast the books that he has
yet to write—he is sixty-five—is that which gave us
the tenderness of *Le Livre de Mon Ami*, and the
spacious sadness of the best pages of *Le Jardin
d'Epicure*. M. France will not spend his last years,
as Taine did, "reading Marcus Aurelius as a sort of
liturgical exercise." Epicure of emotions that he is,
and that was Brunetière's judgment against him, he
will act on taste and not on any principle. That he
will choose his own road is certain; let us hope that
this man, whose every page if not a European event
(and what page now is?) is at least a shining
masterpiece of style, will choose the high road.

INTERNATIONAL SOCIALISTS

STUTTGART, *September* 1907.

I merely strayed into Stuttgart. The high peaks of the Dolomites, and the higher prices of Salzburg —Salt City, without the Lake—have faded into history. The Munich Alp-tourists, who had lain back, limply mountainous, in the corners, showing in the flame of their faces and their peeling skins the brand of glacier-sunshine, have "steiged" heavily out of their native city, where pictures and potations will soon undo the severities of the holiday season. You have passed Augsburg, where somebody confessed his insuperable objections to Confession. You have drunk a crowded and unseemly beer at Ulm. And you are in Stuttgart. . . .

The Congress is going on in the Liederhalle, a combined restaurant and concert-hall. As one sits here in the garden, under an absolute stillness of chestnuts and acacias, it is hard to imagine so much of life as there is in the undistinguished building. Two or three delegates walk up and down, smoking and meditating. A door-keeper leans on the bar counter, under red-and-black and red-and-yellow streamers, and drinks cool, dark beer. A far-from-tidy Fraulein crunches her leisurely way across the gravel to take your order. Another has fallen asleep, her head leaned back against a beech trunk. In the lines of her face there comes out, as often in sleep, a certain forlornness, a sense of defeated dreams. It is a commentary. There are brown and twisted leaves on the gravel; and on state-creeds and state-crafts, too, there comes the inevitable autumn.

But in which of all the Utopias, smouldering in certain fierce eyes that met yours to-day in Stuttgart, will there be no stain of the burden and sorrow of women? If one never got tired, one would always be with the revolutionaries, the re-makers, with Fourier, and Kropotkin. Bnt the soul's energy is straitly limited; and with weariness there comes the need for compromise, for "machines," for repetition, for routine. Fatigue is the beginning of political wisdom.

Those who read the papers know fairly well the resolutions, or, rather, theses, to which the Congress said "Aye." To an actual spectator the dominant note was that of realism. Here and there the vague music of a passionate revolt and an impossible redemption broke out, as when Rosa Luxemburg, clutching her plaid shawl, called up the bloody ghosts of Russian comrades in judgment on the weak "good-sense" of the Congress. But most of the speakers submitted to the strict discipline of fact. Kautsky opposed the demand for the legal establishment of a minimum wage. A powerful argument was led to show that if you establish a minimum wage it tends to operate as a maximum. "Yes!" said Ellenbogen, of Austria. "Theoretically your position is a strong one. Ten years ago I should have voted for it. But since then we have made the experiment in practice. A minimum wage of four francs a day has been established in Zurich, and it has not operated as a maximum."

The Swiss delegates accepted the statement of fact, and at once the Congress swung over to the side of Ellenbogen. "Practical!" cried Vaillant. "You are practical enough. Our programme was once a gospel of enthusiasm. Now it is a party machine, a war-chest, a game of tactics."

In effect this was the dominant tone. The only vote that rang in discord with it was that in favour of the resolution condemning the whole work of colonization as intrinsically and irredeemably bad. This decision was a genuine surprise. Bebel, Vollmar, Bernstein, the English and Americans, all declared against it, but it was, nevertheless, carried. An analysis of the majority drew attention to another characteristic of the Congress—the dominance of the national idea. Bebel and Bernstein were sufficiently clear on this point. The constitution of the Congress was based on a recognition of it. In the old International which was created by Marx, and afterwards, with the teeth of Bakunin, ate Marx up, you had thorough, abstract internationalism. The workers were affiliated directly with the central committee. But with the Congress of 1907 they were affiliated only through the medium of their national organizations.

This raises another question. What will be the binding-power and practical value of the Stuttgart resolutions? Are not those who claim that a complete synthesis of nationalism and internationalism has been effected a little premature? Colonization and colonies stank in the nostrils of the Stuttgart Congress. But will Mr. Ramsay MacDonald in the House of Commons and Herr Bebel in the Reichstag act upon that decision?

As a spectacle, a masque of personalities, the Congress lives in one's memory. It may be a superficial point of view, but it was irresistible. The marvellous interpreters! Whenever anyone speaks they must speak, and they have spoken for five days without growing hoarse.

Of course, there were complaints. Vaillant complained; Vandervelde ascribed the feud between the Labour Party and the S. D. F. to the difficulty of rendering " Klassenkampf " in English. Quelch was verbally mistranslated, before being geographically translated. And there was the Indian Princess.

Hyndman has a long beard, which is a considerable dramatic asset. One still sees him shaking his hands and shouting at Singer, who—large, broad, and with a slight air of the police official—swings the Presidential bell back and forth, to the horror and final collapse of all ears. And Hervé, standing on the table so that all the world might see him, voting for the majority's antimilitarist resolution "with both hands." It must not be thought that the proceedings were in the least tumultuous. They were vehement, but then there is always the House of Commons. By the way, everybody smoked at will in the hall, and one saw many delegates drinking beer at their tables.

Is there a definite, Socialist way of dressing? The red tie has long since gone over to museums and to popular novels. The fluid felt hat is not at all universal. Does anything remain? Well, there is Hervé, in a curious tunic buttoned tight up to the throat, and trousers which bag in an unprecedented way as he hurries along, gesticulating with his knees. But there is no exclusive, Socialist dress.

" Do you think," I asked a newspaper man in the Hotel Royal—the English delegates were having a concert there, and you heard the chorus rolled heavily out through their door—

> Let cowards flinch, and traitors fear,
> We'll keep the Red Flag flying here—

"do you think that the Congress has been of much use " " It will do more to guarantee the peace of the world," he said, "than twenty Hague Conferences. If everybody could afford to travel, there would be no wars. People would discover their neighbours to be so remarkably human. Besides, I am grateful to Stuttgart for not taking it out of us. At the Hague I paid £22 a month for two rooms in a private house.

The Brazilian delegation left their hotel because they were charged £34 a day for four rooms. Peace hath its voracities no less redoubtable than war."
I cannot better his words. Stuttgart did not raise its prices. And when you had swept away preconceptions and prejudices, you found International Socialism unexpectedly human—human, above all, in its fundamental mistake.

A FRENCHMAN'S IRELAND[1]

[1] This study appears as the Introduction to the English version of *L'Irlande Contemporaine*, by M. Paul-Dubois, published under the title of *Contemporary Ireland* (Maunsel & Co., Dublin).

It is the French that have come closest to the secret of Ireland. De Beaumont, that great pupil of De Tocqueville, in 1839, Cardinal Perraud in 1869, painted our national life with the authoritative brush of masters. In addition to these we have had an unbroken line of studies, sketches, and monographs in which Daryl, Béchaux, Le Roz, Fournier, Schindler, Potez, Filon, Flach, De Lavergne, and a cloud of other witnesses have said their word. Edouard Rod shaped the personal tragedy of Parnell into a novel; and in one of his most recent stories Paul Bourget has shuddered at the dresses of fashionable Dublin, and yielded with lyrical abandon to the drowsy and purple magic of the Western lotus-land. M. Paul-Dubois finds one-half of the explanation of this old alliance in history, and the other in likeness of blood and temperament. In exchange for the swords of the Wild Geese, France sent us back priests, or at least the learning that turned Irish boys into priests. She sent too, in later and not less disastrous years, Hoche and Humbert ; and both nations have good memories, and until a very little while ago they shared a common hatred. This Irish mind is, moreover, like the French, "lucid, vigorous and positive," though less methodical, since it never had the happiness to undergo the Latin discipline. France and Ireland have been made to understand each other.

THE DAY'S BURDEN

M. Paul-Dubois, then, has the advantage of temperamental sympathy, wise forerunners, and a long tradition. He had, further, the advantage of language, for it is perhaps only in French that Sociology can become scientific without ceasing to be human. His personal equipment is of the first order. Son of the late President of the Acadèmie des Beaux-Arts, son-in-law of the great Taine, and himself one of the chief officials of the Cour des Comptes, he is a member of the group which Brunetière's erudite enthusiasm gathered round the *Revue des Deux Mondes.* Was it not Taine who originated the phrase "well-documented," and made it the touchstone of all books dealing with social or historical science? At all events it is in that spirit of thoroughness that M. Paul-Dubois has wished to write. The extent of his reading may be gathered from the references in his foot-notes. He paid more than one visit to Ireland, and had he but met some member of the Irish Party—of which he writes with a harshness that is constantly in contradiction with itself—he might fairly claim to have met everybody. The Irish reader of his book may not be in entire agreement with his conclusions. To someone armed with special knowledge on this subject, his exposition may seem inadequate; to someone moved by special passion on that subject, his criticism may even prove an irritant; but, when all is said, his five hundred crowded pages represent the attempt of a mind, at once scientific and imaginative, to see Ireland steadily, and to see it whole. If it is comforting to be understood, it is also of some profit to be misunderstood in a friendly way. M. Paul-Dubois confesses on our behalf no sins that someone or other has not already shouted from the housetops. Whatever he may have to say of the internal life of Ireland, his verdict on the international issue is given clearly and definitely for

94

A FRENCHMAN'S IRELAND

Ireland and against England. His voice is raised
for the Gaelic League, and against linguistic
Imperialism; for the ploughed field, and against
the grazing ranch; for Home Rule, and against
the Act of Union. One may wish to enter a *caveat*
against this or that contention, but the book is
founded not on prejudice, or unreasoned feeling,
or raw idealism, but on a broad colligation of facts;
and, with all reserves made, I believe that it will in
due time take rank with the great studies of modern
communities like Bodley's "France" and Münster-
berg's "The Americans."

What, then, is the Irish Question as seen by this
sociologist, so inspired and so equipped? It is "an
extreme case of social pathology," an instance of
the phenomenon called arrested development. It
is to history that one naturally turns for proof and
illustration of this thesis; and if, as a great Shake-
spearean critic has said, tragedy is simply waste,
the history of Ireland as it passes before us in M.
Paul-Dubois' Introduction, marshalled in sombre
and picturesque lines, is essential tragedy indeed.
It matters nothing whether we approach it in the
spirit of those who desire revenge or of those who
desire reconstruction: the impression is the same.
A civilization shaken by Norse invasion before it
had quite ripened; swept by Anglo-Norman invasion
before it had quite recovered; a people plunged in
an unimaginable chaos of races, religions, ideas,
appetites, and provincialisms; brayed in the mortar
without emerging as a consolidated whole; tenacious
of the national idea, but unable to bring it to triumph;
riven and pillaged by invasion without being conquered—how could such a people find leisure to
grow up, or such a civilization realize its full
potentialities of development and discipline? There
are writers who would have us burn our Irish
Histories. But the historical method imposes itself,

not out of political passion, but by a mere scientific necessity, upon all students of contemporary social, or, indeed, spiritual problems. What is no doubt important is that the past should be studied by the social reformer not for its own sake but for the sake of the present, and from the point of view of the present. It is by this purpose that M. Paul-Dubois has been guided in his masterly Historical Introduction; and I do not know of any summary of the same length which traces the forces of current Irish life so clearly to their origins, and sets the fabric of fact, by which we are to-day confronted, in such true and vivid perspective. But over and beyond that, his Introduction possesses the interest of literature. The period since the Union has never been outlined with more telling or more human touches. O'Connell, the inventor of that " constitutional agitation " which is now the prime weapon of all democracies, passes away leaving "a great memory but not a great party." Young Ireland affords us the supreme instance of the antithetical temperaments ever to be found in Nationalist politics; Davis, the reformer, inspired by love of Ireland, and Mitchel, the revolutionist, inspired by hatred of England. And so through Famine and Fenianism we come down to the brilliant feebleness of Butt and the icy passion of Parnell, who "had more followers than friends," and to the struggle of the Gaelic Renaissance for "psychological Home Rule."

For this is, in last analysis, what M. Paul-Dubois takes to be the deep malady of Ireland: she has not gained the whole world, but she has come perilously near losing her own soul. A certain laxity of will, a certain mystical scepticism in face of the material world, an eloquence which, in depicting Utopias, exhausts the energy that might better be spent in creating them, a continual tendency to fall back on the alibi of the inner life, make Ireland the Hamlet, or still more, the Rudin of the nations. Is this to say that she is unfit for modern, economic civilization? By no means. M. Paul-Dubois, having sounded every weakness and surveyed every difficulty, ends with the belief that the forces of re-growth will prevail over the process of decay; and that although Ireland's last cards are now on the table, she is capable, if she plays them well, not only of preserving an ancient people but of creating a new civilization.

What is the path to this achievement? First of all, under the present regime, England is the enemy.

If Ireland is to realize herself, she must become mistress of her own hearth, her own purse, and her own cupboard. She does assuredly stand in urgent need of peace from politics, and so far her Unionist critics are right. There is indubitably a deep sense in which a nation's life begins where her politics end. People speak as if the outcry against Parliamentarianism were a novel and a unique thing. But, fifty years ago, Marx taught all realists to crack the shells of political formulas and parties and judge them by the moral and economic kernel within. To-day you can pick up anywhere in Paris or Brussels half-a-dozen pamphlets called "The Crisis of Parliamentarianism," "The Absurdity of Parliamentarianism," or "The End of Parliamentarianism." But that peace from the purely political struggle, which is so indispensable if Ireland is to develop character and create material wealth, can come to her only as a result of political autonomy. Until autonomy is won—carrying with it a re-adjustment of taxation—"on the cause must go." And the politicians who keep it going, whatever their special party or tactics, are playing the part of economic realists quite as effectively as any worker on the land or at the loom.

M. Paul-Dubois naturally devotes many chapters to the Land Question. He rightly treats it as a complexus of three questions—the tenure, the distribution, and the use of the land. The first two are being solved, in a fashion, at the cost of Irish taxes, and by the pledging of Irish rates, by the Estates Commissioners and the Congested Districts Board. Landlordism is dying, and dying meanly, "its last thought being of a bargain to be made." The edifice of Feudalism is being dismantled at a cost that raises a very real menace of national bankruptcy, but at all events the grim walls are coming down. But while the liberation of the Irish countryside from landlordism was necessary, it is not sufficient. The farmer must learn to use his land productively; and so there must be a great development of agricultural education, leading up to a general system of "mixed farming." The Department of Agriculture must therefore be a prime concern of a self-governing Ireland. He must learn to combine; and in this respect, at least as regards the small holders, Co-operation possesses the secret of the future. He must come free of the egoism and pessimism which have remained in his blood since the Great Famine; and nothing can expel these except the singing and dancing Gaelic League. But, even with all this accomplished, he will still be a snake-strangled Laocoon until he has in some wise reformed and mastered his Railways and Banks.

When we turn to the industrial condition of the country we find, since the Union, a steady degeneration of economic tissue. Population doubles between 1800 and 1841, but manufacture decays. The cotton workers of Belfast fall in number within that period from 27,000 to 12,000; and the factory hands of Dublin from 4,938 to 682. The consumption of luxuries, an excellent test of wealth, shows an immediate decline, tobacco falling in thirty years by

37 per cent. and wine by 47 per cent. Loss of trade follows loss of the flag. London, having become the political centre of gravity of Ireland, tends also to become her financial and commercial centre of gravity. There is a diminution of the productive, and a great increase of the parasitic classes. The home market slips away from the home manufacturer; a sort of mania of exchange takes possession of the country; and she imports much that she might produce at home, and exports much that she might consume at home, paying ruinous tribute on both processes to the Shylocks of transit. It is a situation too sadly familiar to us all. M. Paul-Dubois' remedy, too, is familiar; it is the programme of the men of 1779 and of the Industrial Pioneers of to-day. Use at home as many as you need of the things that are made at home, and make at home as many as possible of the things that are used at home. He neither anticipates nor desires any notable development of industry on the great scale, but looks for the prosperity of Ireland to progressive agriculture, and the smaller rural industries that come naturally to cluster around it.

Such is, in bare outline, the diagnosis of Ireland made by this detached and sympathetic student. He touches upon many other subjects, upon that of Clericalism and Anti-Clericalism, with particular delicacy and insight. One may regret that, with his French experience, he does not discuss such problems as that now rising very definitely on the political horizon: Does Ireland stand to gain or to lose by Protection? One may find a fault of line or of colour here and there, or chance on an irritating phrase. But on the whole and as a whole this is the best book that has been written in recent years on the problems of Ireland. The meaner journalism may seek in it for nothing better than party capital. But the worker in any Irish movement, who possesses the supreme wisdom of humility, and who had rather be bettered than flattered, will be glad to have seen himself in M. Paul-Dubois' mirror. His last message is one of hope. He may, as his Conclusion shows, have under-rated the resolution of Ireland to secure integral Home Rule—a National Government being a delicate and intricate machine which cannot be set working in halves. He may, by times, have seemed to forget that there are many kinds of Conciliation, that, for instance, an infalliable method of conciliating a tiger is to allow oneself to be devoured. But, as between us and our rulers, he gives his verdict, on the evidence, for Ireland and against England. And he foreshadows a possible unification of all progressive parties on the Irish side, a tacit Concordat under which, on the sole condition that the national idea be not submerged or the national flag lowered in surrender, all progressive parties would come to regard themselves as but different regiments of the same Army of Advance. May that hope come true!

ON SAYING GOOD-BYE

The smell of the sea, so raw and stringent in a
landsman's nostrils, brings thoughts with it and a
strange spume of memories. To me it brings a perception of what people mean when they toss in the
air that dusty adjective, "cynical." A cynic is a
man who, finding himself, for all striving, incurably
sad from the lips in, sets himself to be incorrigibly gay
from the lips out. It is a triumph of will over
temperament, a way of courage, and, by times, even
a way of nobleness.

So it appears to me at least with the wash of the
river about the brattling boat. But why should
cables and gangways, cranes and the throb of steam,
waved white handkerchiefs and all that apparatus
of adieu, set anyone framing definitions of "cynicism"? It is because a dead Frenchman, who had
not wit enough even to keep himself from being
forgotten, a cynic as they say, one Brizeux, murmurs
to himself in one of his comedies as I murmur to
myself every time I leave Ireland: "Do not cry
out against *la patrie*. Your native land after all will
give you the two most exquisite pleasures of your
life, that of leaving her and that of coming back."
He left many other sharp sentences along his way,
but I only remember that of Cécile after she had
transferred her affections. "And to think that six
months ago I loved Alphonse! Mon Dieu! How
he has changed!"

There are no taxis in my native city of Dublin.
But the depressed jarvey who drove me to the
North Wall knows that they are coming. He starts
already in his dreams at the hoot of their horns.

You cannot stand against science, he says: look at
Corbett, and Tommy Burns, and Johnson. A man
can't get bread at it nowadays, although, of course,
"when a body meets a free-spoken, free-handed
gentleman like yourself, sir; none o' these mane
divils that'd be resthrictin' you to your legal fare,
mind you. . . ." The electric trams were bad
enough, but this other would be the end. The
Merrion Square doctors were good friends of the
poor man, would think nothing of taking your car
for two or three hours and leaving a sovereign in your
palm, but first one got a motor, and now they all have
motors. What is one to say?

A member of Parliament ought to be a minister
of consolation, at all events in matters of livelihood.
All that occurs to me to tell my driver is that he is
an element in an interesting transition in the organization of transport. The domestication of horses
created him and his tribe, the domestication of petrol
is in course of blotting them out. Mr. Galsworthy
will write a play on the subject and make us quiver
unhelpfully; and there is always the workhouse
coffin to look to, and an absolutely gratuitous burial.
Meantime, he had better be rehearsing his adieus.
But it seems hardly worth while dropping that oil
into his wounds. There will, one fears, be more
hunger than dignity in his leave-taking. Semi-
starvation, mitigated by a gay heart and an incessant
tongue, will take him, and not gently, by the hand,
and show him, the Way Out. And by way of
monument he shall have, perhaps, the one-ten
millionth part of a paragraph in some economic
history that will be written by some sociologist of
Teutonic extraction.

An old woman, once questioned by a journalist,
declared that the only bothersome thing about
walking was that the miles began at the wrong end.
Kant, who could talk to Time and Space like an

equal, is dead, and so nobody will ever know what the old lady meant. I record the observation here merely because it sounds so horribly intelligent.

But there is a constant heart-break in travel which comes from this that every departure is a sort of geographical suicide. To live anywhere even for an hour or a day is to become inwoven into a manifold tissue, material and spiritual. You cannot pluck yourself suddenly out without carrying a fringe of destruction, and it is your own personality that dies in every snapped fibre. Philosophers have thought of the soul as a spiritus—a rapid gust of breath blown along the worlds and quickly dissipated. In truth our conscious life is like a white drift of fog that leaves a vestige of itself clinging to every object that it passes. It is a sustained good-bye. I cannot reach any thought except by leaving another. Even so common and kindly an experience as dinner is not exempt from this spiritual succession duty: your coffee is bitter with the unspoken adieus of the soup, and the fish, and the fowl, and the roast over whose graves you have marched to fulfilment. Life is a cheap table d'hôte in a rather dirty restaurant, with Time changing the plates before you have had enough of anything.

We were bewildered at school to be told that walking was a perpetual falling. But life is, in a far more significant way, a perpetual dying. Death is not an eccentricity, but a settled habit of the universe. The drums of to-day call to us, as they call to young Fortinbras in the fifth act of *Hamlet*, over corpses piled up in such abundance as to be almost ridiculous. We praise the pioneer, but let us not praise him on wrong grounds. His strength lies not in his leaning out to new things—that may be mere curiosity—but in his power to abandon old things. All his courage is a courage of adieus.

The romance of travel appealed to many in old

days, and now, after menace of extinction, it has
been conclusively restored by the Tariff Reform
deputations. Others were light enough to think that
no one can travel without striking one day upon the
path of wisdom. But this cannot altogether be
granted. We Leinstermen used to hit off the
idealism of distance in a proverb : " All the cows
in Connaught have long horns." Clarence Mangan
was of the same mind :

> Moor, Egyptian, Persian, Turk and Roman
> Thread one common downhill path of doom ;
> Everywhere the word is man and woman,
> Everywhere the old sad sins find room.

But Brizeux cuts deeper when he shows that the
true value of going away is that it enables one to
come back. I once knew a man who was commis-
sioned by a railway company to write a booklet on
the attractions of certain towns, among others, Xyz.
He produced this page : "Attractions of Xyz. Print
here in large type all the trains by which it is
possible to leave Xyz." He was a native of it. and
in such a light must one's native place sometimes
appear. You burn to break the monotone with a
great shout, to shake its trivial dust off your feet, to
strain to yours the throbbing bosom of life, to mix
brooks and stars and art and love and youth into one
crashing orchestra of experience. And then, when
you have taken this wide way, you find yourself
burning to come back to that native place of yours
where, as you now remember, the water was more
cordial than wine, and the women sweeter than
angels.

There is only one journey, as it seems to me, in
this inweaving of parables and facts, in which we
attain our ideal of going away and going home at
the same time. Death, normally encountered, has
all the attractions of suicide without any of its

horrors. The old woman when she comes to that road will find the miles beginning at the right end. We shall all bid our first real adieu to those brother-gaolers of ours, Time and Space; and though the handkerchiefs flutter, no lack of courage will have power to cheat or defeat us. "However amusing the comedy may have been," wrote Pascal, "there is always blood in the fifth act. They scatter a little dust on your face; and then all is over for ever." Blood there may be, but blood does not necessarily mean tragedy. The wisdom of humility bids us pray that in that fifth act we may have good lines and a timely exit; but, fine or feeble, there is comfort in breaking the parting word into its two significant halves, à Dieu. Since life has been a constant slipping from one good-bye into another, why should we fear that sole good-bye which promises to cancel all its fore-runners?

1910.

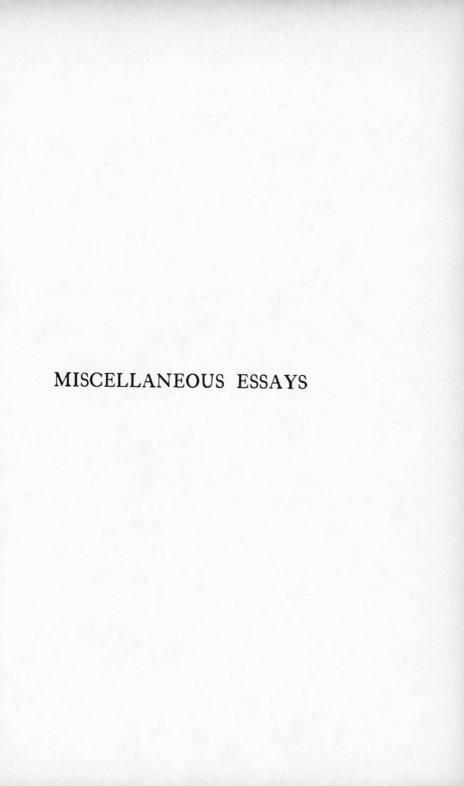

MISCELLANEOUS ESSAYS

LABOUR AND CIVILIZATION

The dogmatic mantle has long since fallen out of fashion among economists. That too pushing omniscience, once imputed to the tribe by satirists, angers nobody now; it exists only as a memory of veterans. Economics is no longer presented as an integral, or even a partial, Rule of Life: if the modern masters of the science are guilty of any sin in that regard, it is an excessive reluctance in counsel. The critic complains, if at all, of their remoteness and detachment. They have organized too well their escape from real life, some into history, some into the serene shadow-land of mathematics.

This attitude reflects through a special medium the mind of the community. It is doubtful whether there were ever before in the world at any moment so many honest, bewildered men. We feel, most of us, as much astray and amazed as a peasant suddenly plunged into the clamour of dynamos, or into that of the Stock Exchange, The twentieth century, which cuts such a fine figure in encyclopædias, is most familiarly known to the majority of its children as a new sort of headache. And its moral burden is felt to be unbearable. In a simple social organization, justice is an ideal that carries straight to the mark. It is constantly reinforced by obvious fulfilment. It does not get lost on the way. But in our vast and unimaginable maze of interdependent processes and reactions, mere honesty comes to appear to the discouraged mind as the laudable, but entirely fruitless, caprice of a cipher. Any personal attempt to redress the balance of distribution is commonly regarded as either a freak, an imperti-

nence, a nullity, or a betrayal. Raise voluntarily the
wages of your workmen, and you are "branded" as
a traitor to your class. Improve factory conditions
that fall within your own control, and you are
denounced for a subtle intrigue against the loyalty of
your workers to their class. You are gilding the oats
of servitude for your slaves. Intervene in a strike
with an appeal for peace, and you become a Derby
dog for the contempt and the missiles of both parties
to the quarrel. Try to give a penny to a poor
woman outside the church door after Mass, and all
civilization is mobilized to prevent such a horror.
Adhere to the opposite view that salvation is only of
a committee, that everything must be anonymous,
departmentalized, and even State-managed, and you
are in no better case. Oppose the Insurance Act,
for instance, and Mr. Masterman characterizes you
as a thick-hided and miserly individualist. Accept
it, and Mr. Belloc trounces you as a hireling prophet,
and forerunner of the Servile State. Tolerate or
even explain Mr. Larkin, and you are a mad,
contract-breaking anarchist. Support Mr. Ramsay
Macdonald against him, and you are either a crawling
fusionist and trimmer, or, in the alternative, the dupe
of a wrecker, who is all the more dangerous because
of his smooth and plausible ways.

I do not wish to exaggerate, but it is a fact of
daily experience that many a fine straightness of
purpose is getting itself twisted in the confusion of
the times. The violent splutter of adjectives which
passes for social philosophy, not only among the
untrained missionaries of discontent but also among
the well-trained orthodox, is admirably calculated to
produce that spiritual nausea which we call cynicism.
Not a little of the restless end even desperate
frivolity, which is deplored as the characteristic vice
of the age, may be traced to that source. Many
people, and not always the worst, feel sincerely that

they have minds equal to the task of taking the world flippantly, but not equal to anything more serious. They turn with hectic enthusiasm to Auction Bridge and the Tango, partly because they cannot find a key to the graver business of civilization. They are not enemies to the light, but merely aliens. They will tell you that they are not on the road to Damascus largely because they cannot find it, and the excuse will not be without a certain tinge or infiltration of truth. The road upon which they are is, in truth, paved with good intentions: one can see that, and, dazed by the contention of the guides, can understand the weariness that unshouldered baggage so awkward.

Such is the psychology of some part at least of our *fainéance*. The remainder is not so respectable in its origins, and neither imagines itself nor is imagined to be anything more complex than the static inertia of comfort. But that there is sincere trouble of mind among men of goodwill may be taken as beyond question. It is palpably there, it is real, and it is so deeply and variously rooted in everyday conditions as to be difficult even to reach with any hope of dispersal. But there is nothing to justify the throwing up of impotent hands. Impossibilism is a poor word and an unmanly doctrine. We have got to keep moving on, and, since that is so, we had better put as good thought as we can into our itinerary. The task of civilization was never easy. Freedom—the phrase belongs to Fichte, or to someone of his circle—has always been a battle and a march: it is of the nature of both that they should appear to be the participants, during the heat of movement, as planless and chaotic. The Bill Adamses do in fact win the Waterloo of history, but they do not know how. It is their sons, pouring over picture books, who grasp the tactical integrity of the affair, and their grandsons who understand its human significance. Whatever else economic life may be, it is of late very plainly a battle. But no such lapse of time is now needed for comprehension : it explains itself as it goes on. The policy of labour is no longer an eyeless, instinctive groping ; it is a mature and self-conscious campaign. It has its definite goal, its metaphysics, its very sophisticated poetry. The rest of society has undergone a similar mental transformation. It has acquired the faculty of doubling the roles of actor and spectator. It has at hand information not before available as to conditions of life. In short it is able, although not without an effort, to rationalize its development, and to elect between the alternatives posed in practical conflict.

In the perplexity spoken of there is probably a considerable leaven of self-deception. The dead weight of details overwhelms us, largely because we lack the courage of the obvious. We are muscle-bound, not precisely by downright egotism or dullness, but by that unaccountable palsy, sometimes experienced, in which mind and brain seem to be cloven into unrelated halves. The goads of economic life we grasp with one half of ourselves as the grossest of platitudes ; the responsive kicks and twitchings are regarded by the other half as a dark and evil paradox. The simple truth is that, in contemporary conditions, what we call the Labour Unrest is just as normal as pain in disease. There is a proved discord between the business order of things on the one part, and the human order on the other. Our industrial system clashes not only with ethical, but even with physiological requirements. Thirty per cent. of our whole population dwell just on or just below the hunger line, and local or seasonal disadvantages depress a great body of them to a level even lower. Our contemporary age,

if marked out in the calendar by its humane enthusiasms, is also unhappily marked out by rising prices.
If the worker is pinched and cramped in respect of
those two fundamentals, food and clothing, his
relation to the third, shelter, is even more abject.
The plenitude of large-scale production, and power
transport, has cheapened wheat and woollens much
more effectively than it has cheapened houses. It
is not only in Dublin that the *damnosa haereditas* of
the slum curtains the cradle of the poor with its
misery and its defilement. All this we know very
well : we repeat it over and over till it becomes
almost an idle tale, and the next moment we are
crying out with astonishment at some fresh strike.
That is not a wise, or even an intelligible attitude.
The first principle to lay firm hold on, as it seems
to me, is the causal bond between want and unrest.
The continual heel-flingings of which we complain
are really reflex rather than deliberate. It will
further be discovered to be a sound, though a rough,
working-clue to assume that all strikes are the same
strike. If we are to master the situation at all we
must think of the worker not as a unit in a Board
of Trade table, nor yet as a nihilist, a metaphysician,
or a prophet. Taking him as we find him, we are,
especially in these countries, in presence of a man
concrete in temper almost to the point of earthiness.
He offers the most unpromising material for a
chapter in demonology. Not only does he prefer
peace to war, but he even prefers work to idleness.
No other man in the state accepts so stoutly the
discipline of incessant striving, or savours so heartily
the frugal comforts and common pleasures of
existence. Let me not seem to suggest the absurd
and belittling notion that he is devoid of idealism.
Certain of his theorists have indeed constantly
treated him as a mere resultant of appetites; but
a Catholic at least knows that, at his highest,

he has been the guardian and keeper of the shrine. But he is a man who lives, if the phrase be allowed, very close to life, and very far away from all species of cloudy architecture. His revolutions are essentially revolutions of the kitchen cup-board. In substance, if not in technical form, his *émeutes* all relate back to such tremendous simplicities as that. When he rises against the dismissal of a Driver Knox, for instance, he is not concerned in the least to assert what some of his Corinthians have formulated as the divine right to get drunk outside business hours. Nor is it the core of his grievance that the frontiers of his leisure have been violated, or that his social habits have been subjected to criticism. It is that any rash or fussy person, set in authority, has the power to call into action against him, suddenly and on any lightest pretext, good or bad, that armoury of which the chief weapon is starvation. When a Trade Union is fighting for recognition, a very brief inquiry will show you that the typical combatant is not, in the last analysis, very passionately interested in the abstract or the remote. He regards his organization not as a piece of grandiose mythology, after the fashion of a Pouget, a Sorel, or even a Larkin, but as a known and definite mode of putting or keeping wages up.

Side by side with this practical tradition, ambient about it like a sort of astral body, there is also of course the metaphysical tradition of labour. That is, in some of its phases, visionary and sinister enough to justify the most picturesque of nightmares. In its place it merits the most careful study. But with the ordinary striker, or "unrestful" worker it has very little to do. And that is a very fortunate circumstance. The great task of to-day is to rally the worker to civilization. If the panic-pictures of him were true, that would be an impossible task. If it were true that the worker really desired to end the present organization of society, there is no power on earth that could balk, or even long postpone, his passage from will to deed. You could not invoke against him the authority of Parliament, for in democratic states he is the majority that creates and could control Parliament. Nor could you appeal to force, for he is the police, the army and the navy. The fact is so obvious as to demand no elaboration. It forms the ground-work of what is perhaps the most lyrical invitation, and at the same time the angriest rebuke in all the prophetic books of revolutionism. But the prophets of overthrow are altogether wrong in believing that the quiescence of labour is due to the apathy of habit, to lack of imagination, or to cowardice. The worker will not make an end of civilization simply because he is himself a civilized man. He feels— for it is feeling rather than logic—that there is in our system of private ownership, despite everything, a sort of bedrock fitness and necessity. The justice towards which he is groping is there, if not in actuality at any rate as a *ratio seminalis*. Scientific control of nature is there, adequate, if it be but guided by common sense and good will, to the con-quest of destitution. Scope is there for the play of personality; and to a man, whose unrealized ambitions cry out anew for fulfilment in his children, that is by no means the least virtue of our system. The worker is already rallied to the idea, to the schematic essence of our Western civilization. Our task is to rally him to its actual shape by so trans-forming that latter, as given to us by the accidents of history, that it shall be fit for the habitation of the idea.

Some apology should perhaps be offered for such an italicizing of the obvious. But if a landscape is, as has been said, a state of mind, a society is, in an even deeper sense, a state of mind or rather of will. One of the effects of terror with some people is to make them shut their eyes: it is a duty of those of us who, although frightened, are not so badly frightened, to give evidence as to the nature of the things we see.

If the foregoing analysis is, in its main lines, correct, it follows that there is not much matter to be learned from a minute consideration of recent upheavals such as those of Dublin, and, on a smaller scale, of Leeds. There was something Byronic about the Dublin struggle: it taught us little, but we undoubtedly "felt it like a thunder-roll." No note of the whole scale of melodrama was absent. Patriotism and bread-and-butter, bread-and-butter and religion, religion and economic solidarity, nationalism and internationalism, diplomacy and war, the catastrophic method and the gradual, dictatorship and democracy, and one knows not how many other great ideas were clashed against one another in arbitrary and hopeless antithesis. Stones, batons, nearly all the pomp and all the not infrequent absurdity of the law, secret councils, processions, amazing perorations, epigrams that were veritable wads of gun-cotton, disguises, slayings, arrests, and escapes—it was all in the mode not merely of melodrama, but of the cinema theatre. It is in the nature of a very miserable destiny that everything that happens in Ireland, from a public banquet to a private funeral, should be seized on as affording a conclusive reason against Home Rule, the Catholic hierarchy, the Gaelic League, the Gulf Stream or some other of our special iniquities. It is hardly necessary to say that the Dublin strike proved to a large number of enthusiastic writers that all their worst fears, and their best hopes, on both sides of all questions affecting our future were more than justified. The serious significance of it is perhaps best reached in a less confident way. By a strange paradox it was at once the most individual, and the most general of all recent outbreaks. Of all the great cities of the United Kingdom, Dublin is the weakest in economic structure. It is a capital of government officials, professional men, annuitants; its wealth, such as it is, is concentrated in those classes which the popular mind, untruly and yet not fantastically, regards as parasitical. Their incomes are drawn not from the volume of local production, but from that larger stream of national production which is tributary to their specialized pursuits, though not to others. The business world is occupied chiefly with carrying and commerce, very little with manufacture. The great body of the workers are engaged in low-wage occupations. Not less than one-fourth of the population is constantly below the human minimum. Housing is particularly bad, the "poor street" being in the typical instance a decayed "good street," planned originally for other uses and wholly unsuitable to that to which it has come. The labour propaganda had hardly reached the mass of the unskilled: organization was almost unknown to them. On this terrain appeared suddenly the disturbing personality of Mr. Larkin. Picturesque, eloquent, prophetic, at once dictatorial and intimate, he was, as he might say himself, the very man for the job. The Dublin worker is not a natural revolutionary, but he is a natural soldier. Mr. Larkin, appealing at once to all his instincts, organized not so much a Union as an army. In a long series of attacks, the main strength of which resided in the fact that they were sudden and concentrated on a single employer or group of employers, he won much oftener than he lost. His opponents were taken by surprise. In many instances they had but a very poor defence: wages were not only under the human minimum, but in some trades they were clearly lower than business could bear, and they had not, for an unduly long time, shown any improvement. In all cases the employers were inadequately trained to modern methods of industrial diplomacy. Without quite knowing what they were about, they allowed themselves to be manœuvred into an apparent challenge to the fundamental principle of Trade Unionism. Both in argument, and in conflict, they failed very notably to hold their own. A condition of day-to-day menace and insecurity was created; no employer, sitting down to his correspondence in the morning, felt certain that his men would not be called out by telephone before the dinner-hour. But among the employers also the idea of solidarity began to germinate. They, too, by one of those chances or ordinations that supply most of the interest of history, found a leader of the requisite type at the crucial momemt. Mr. William Murphy is a humane man, known for his personal honour and charity; a "good employer" as it is called, a successful captain of enterprise, an insensitive imagination, in short, a very dangerous opponent. Under his impulsion they consolidated their forces. How far the process of federation went, what was the nature of its financial basis, what subventions, if any, it received from the English federated employers we do not know. But these facts, if known, would furnish us with the master-key to the course of the struggle. What is evident is that when the Dublin committee declared that they had made up their minds "to smash Larkinism" and to drive him out of the capital as he had been driven out of Belfast, Cork and Wexford, they were not spinning phrases. They were talking by the most influential of all books, the bank-book. They threatened, and they performed.

The sense in which the Dublin struggle was strongly individual, provoked and controlled by things local and not universal, will appear from this rough

analysis. But we have to note further that it came
at a point of crisis in the history of labour. The
critics of Parliamentarianism, the apostles of direct
action, of economic as contrasted with political
pressure, found in the fighting spirit of the Dublin
worker an asset and an opportunity irresistible to
them. The issues had been posed in such terms
that, on the face of it, the most conservative Trade
Unionist had no choice but to support the men.
With the assurance of this solid support, the more
extreme spirits were free to play with fire. The
class-war was preached in whirling superlatives.
The force of gutter-journalism, on both sides, could
no further go. It was a humiliation to read in one
column the noblest appeal to justice or to order, and,
in the next, to come on a personal irrelevant foulness,
as of a well wantonly choked with garbage. Nobody
wants to be a prude or a dandy in these matters, but
the mud which besmears impartially the flinger of it,
and his target, is not a contribution to human progress. A dramatic demonstration was given of the
triumph of class solidarity over racial, religious and
even geographical division : at least that was how
the affair appeared to the Syndicalist " rebel chiefs."
Behind it all the civic organism, within which the
duel had been joined, displayed every symptom of a
very real distress. The workers fought with admirable courage : there was very little drinking or
violence and a great deal of idealism and soldierly
sacrifice. But there is a point beyond which the belt
cannot be tightened. The English labour officials
repudiated what they regarded as the reckless and
impossible strategy of Mr. Larkin, and cut off supplies.
The employers, on their part, carried out with
resolution and success their programme of " fighting
to a finish." They rejected with open contempt all
attempts at conciliatory intervention by a Citizens'
Peace Committee, overturning Lord Mayors, Privy

Councillors, Deans, doctors and professors like disregarded ninepins. They glanced at Sir George Askwith's Dublin Castle Report, and pitched it forthwith in the fire. In these circumstances there could be only one issue. We are left with an extremely ambiguous state of affairs. The dispute has not come to a conclusion, it has merely stopped: no settlement has been formulated. In some cases the men have gone back with no questions asked. In the building trades they have signed the obnoxious "document" which proscribes the Transport Union. The carpenters have had served on them a requisition, which so far has been refused, to introduce into their agreement new clauses renouncing the "sympathetic strike," and the doctrine of "tainted goods." There has been plenty of "victimization," and plenty of "desertion." Not less than six thousand strikers are estimated to be still drifting about unemployed. The introduction of motor lorries in large numbers during the dispute has added to other problems that of the displacement of labour by machinery. Not a single member of the submerged fourth seems to be any nearer a living, or as it is now currently called, an economic wage. The Housing Report in increasing knowledge has certainly increased sadness, but, in the absence of Imperial aid such as has been promised to local authorities, we are no closer to a solution.

At the first blush it would seem as if the masters had won all along the line. But they themselves are not quite certain what it is that they have won. People ask, like the mathematician after the play: What does all that prove? What in fact does it prove? It is not a victory over Trade Unionism, for the employers formally declared that they were fighting not Trade Unionism but Mr. Larkin. It is not a failure of the General Strike, or even of the much more limited sympathetic strike: neither was

seriously tried. On this point some explanation is
needed. The sympathetic strike, as understood in
England, is essentially a strike declared by one
Union in support of another. In Dublin the con-
trolling feature was the fact that the Transport
Union was not a specialized trade or craft body, but
a sort of omnibus or hotch-potch organization into
which such diverse elements as biscuit-makers,
tramway-men, and agricultural labourers were
gathered. It might have been founded on that
classic page in which Mill points out that all
economic effort is reducible to the moving of matter
from one place to another. Any collective action
on the part of such a body is bound to hit the community simultaneously at many points. The blows
are more numerous, but there is less weight behind
them. Nobody supposes that things in Dublin
have swung back to anything like stable equilibrium.
Mr. Larkin may go to South Africa, but he will not
take with him the slums, the hunger, or the hope-
lessness of outlook that are the true organizers of
revolution. If there is peace in Dublin it is the
peace of industrial anæmia, not that of a healthy
civilization.

But if no problem has been solved many have
been posed with a new exigence. They are either
local or general, and again they are either mechanical and secondary, or else of that fundamental kind
outlined earlier in this paper. The whole business
future of the Irish capital has been posed as a
problem. You lack the key to it until you understand that Dublin itself is grievously under-
developed, and that it focusses with lamentable
truth the arrested development of the nation as a
whole. The change to a new economic order in this
regard is, for most of us in Ireland, bound up with
the change to a new political order: that, however,
is not a discussion immedlately proper to these

pages. As for more general considerations, we may well style mechanical and secondary all those relating to schemes of arbitration and conciliation. There is no saving virtue in "bringing people together" as the phrase goes: the prize-ring, for instance, brings pugilists together, but the result is not conspicuously peaceful. Everything depends on the philosophy of action behind the lips of the negotiators and on the actual facts of the case. In one point of view all economic inquiries are an unqualified good, namely, as sources of information. In that point of view they must be developed and extended until each half of the world knows exactly how the other half lives. Our knowledge on the subject, although greatly improved of late years, is still inadequate to the point of humiliation. The Board of Trade investigations into wages, rents and prices; the Income Tax and Death Duty returns, the economic importance of which is certainly not inferior to the fiscal; the Census of Production, and a whole range of publications that will come to mind, ought to be conceived not as casual Blue Books but as the germ of a new literature. The Year Books, among which one may signalize particularly the *Year Book of Social Progress* and the *Encyclopædia of Industrialism*, both of which seem to owe their extraordinary usefulness to the inspiration of Professor Ashley; the work of Mr. Chiozza Money, Professor Bowley, Mr. J. A. Hobson, Professor Chapman, Mr. Ramsay Macdonald, and the more responsible Fabians; all the publications of the Catholic Social Guild and especially of Monsignor Parkinson—one mentions only random examples—are not mere books, but the lines of a new social orientation. The Oxford volume on Property, although it is not much more than St. Thomas Aquinas and water, and Mr. Cole's brilliant and dangerous *World of Labour* are significant recent additions. The time has come for the State, which alone commands the authority and the resources, to consolidate the results of all these diverse investigations into one Manual of Citizenship. In so far as Courts of Conciliation which, from the nature of things, must be Courts of Inquiry, help to elicit the actual facts of economic life they should be strongly favoured.

When they are conceived as agencies of peace we enter a new area. The outstanding problem posed by the Dublin employers is that of compulsory arbitration, penally enforceable through the medium of money guarantees. The interest of this proposal can hardly be exaggerated. It challenges, or at any rate, appears to challenge, the present position of Trade Unions before the law, and this is, in effect, to challenge their whole historical achievement. It dismisses the considered report of the Industrial Council, which, be it noted, is a joint and not a sectional Board. They found unanimously (Cd. 6952. 1913) that moral obligation and mutual consent afforded a much stronger guarantee of peace than any legal penalty or prohibition. But what renders the proposal even more interesting is the diminishing disfavour with which compulsory arbitration of some kind is regarded by Parliamentary Socialists like Mr. Ramsay Macdonald and Mr. Snowden. Mr. Crooks has long been known as an advocate of it, and he has been roundly condemned by the Trade Union Congress. But one finds Mr. Cole declaring that the Congress may very likely accept it, if another and less repugnant name can be devised. And in Mr. Macdonald's last book, *The Social Unrest*, one comes upon a suggestive passage:

" . . . the field upon which organized labour can win victories is being so narrowed as to impose a heavy handicap on the workmen. Capital is being concentrated for industrial purposes, and

federated for defensive purposes against Labour
combinations, and organized Capital left to deal
with organized Labour under existing conditions
enters a contest with everything in its favour.
That is the reason why Trade Unionism is turning
its thoughts more and more towards legislation,
and is finding ideas of compulsory arbitration
more and more consistent with that new
position."

It is evident enough that Mr. Macdonald wants
his State to keep the capitalist in order, and that
the Dublin employers want *their* State to keep the
Unions in order. But the question has been posed.
The close federation of employers was visibly
present; its success may very well be a new point
of departure.

In all that has been said it should be clearly
understood that there is no belittlement of the
function of Conciliation Boards. In an atmosphere
of goodwill they may be very valuable aids to peace.
The fact that the Irish bishops have exercised their
immense moral influence towards the establishment
of such bodies in Ireland is of the greatest importance. To say that machinery is not, of its own
inherent magic, adequate to the situation is very
far from saying that it is not, in its place, valuable
and even indispensable. The creation of it,
especially in Dublin, is indeed of all secondary
tasks before us the most urgent.

But it is our social philosophy, and the practical
policy founded on it, that alone can rally the workers
to civilization. The strike must be grasped not
only as a disturbance, and an act of war, but as a
monstrously expensive advertisement of the present
abject condition of labour. Until we have made up
our minds to change that condition we shall only
be padding round in a verbal prison. Let us look

at things in the simplest possible way. The function of an economic system is to feed, clothe, and shelter, in a human way, its human units. Since ours does not accomplish that, we must so amend it that it shall do so. There is no vain dream of an impossible Utopia, and no hope of banishing that part of the mass of destitution which is due to personal malfeasance. But neither should there be a too easy acceptance of things given. The business world as we have inherited it from the exploiters of the great inventions, and their economic counsellors, was not, in its origins, framed on any high ethical model: we may come some day to look back on it not as one of the supreme triumphs, but as one of the strange aberrations of the human spirit. Such is the suggestion of writers so far removed from Communism as the late Arnold Toynbee, and Mr. Hilaire Belloc. In the effort to transform this fabric, we must not think so fantastically well of human nature as to suppose that logic and justice will suffice. There may be need from time to time for the ministration of war: it may be taken for granted that situations will develop out of which no humaner way will appear possible. All the time each economic class will find it necessary so to organize its strength as to exert its appropriate, stabilizing "pull" on the process of distribution. That is the rationale alike of Consumer's Leagues, Co-operatives of all kinds, Employers' Federations, and Trade Unions. Equilibrium between these forces is not to be maintained by mere slackness and resignation: it imposes on the community a strain as constant as the muscular tension of a wire-walking acrobat. Occasional disturbance is, unhappily, lodged as a menace in the very principle of our system. While human beings continue to be born into a sub-human existence, from which only the strongest and the luckiest can hope to escape, our civilization is, so far forth, a contradiction in terms. That must be the material foundation, and the mind of the worker must be the moral foundation of any philosophy of peace. If, on the one hand, the living wage were unattainable, if, when the skeleton went, the feast had to go, or if, on the other, the worker had finally chosen revolution as his trade, the outlook for our world would be hopeless. But although things are bad, they are not so bad as that. What is essential is that the conservative should realize that there must be a great change, and that the extremist should realize that the change can only be gradual. To ignore either condition is to lose hold of the problem. The transformation cannot be catastrophic : even the theorists of Socialism have long since ceased to think in economic Jenas or Sedans. In too many parasitic or casual industries the immediate choice is between bad wages and no wages. To enforce forthwith even a moderate standard would be to drive out all the marginal employers, and to add whole new regiments to the army of unemployment. But to torture these commonplaces into a new Iron Law, to linger on the difficulties and to deprecate the necessity of a changed order, is to have already declared war on the soul of labour. Forbid me to hope for myself, and it is a hard saying but not intolerable : widen that interdiction until you exile eternally from the sun my children, and my children's children, and you make peace nothing better than the drowse of poltroons. There is in our midnight a hidden morrow; if we deliberately commit our energies to the task we can, year by year, and stage by stage, remoralize our society. It is that prospect, and not its actual shape, that will rally to it in faith and action the working class. They are realists, and if they see such a purpose honestly pursued, we need have no fear as to the flag of their election. We must also, as it seems to me, be more discriminate in onr alliances. *Divide*

et impera is a dangerous maxim, and those spokesmen
of orthodoxy who regard it as good tactics to exaggerate every difference of opinion that may chance to
arise in the labour camp, to embroil its various parties,
and to include them all in one impartial condem-
nation, are conspicuously ill-inspired. Where the
cause at issue is personal vanity you may well, as
the phrase goes, "play off" one agitator against
another: but when ultimate human needs come in
question any such effort must be at once mean and
vain. If we find men, whose spiritual orientation
is not altogether ours, marching in the same
direction, we ought to march with them to the
term of our common objective, and not separate
for battle until that term has been reached. Every
voluntary and every State proposal that tends to
broaden the basis of property—co-operation, co-
partnership, prosperity sharing, manufacturing
guilds, taxation of unprotective surpluses—ought
to be welcomed by us. But in the end it is personality that counts. If we are to be saved we must
help in the saving. The great Encyclicals of
Leo XIII, those spacious and noble utterances of
the true social philosophy, bring all our effort to
its inevitable point.

"Every one should put his hand to the work
which falls to his share, and that at once and
straightway, lest the evil which is already so great
become through delay absolutely beyond remedy.
Those who rule the State should avail themselves
of the laws and institutions of the country;
masters and wealthy owners must be mindful of
their duty; the poor, whose interests are at stake,
should make every lawful and proper effort; and
since religion alone . . . . can avail to destroy
the evil at its root, all men should rest persuaded
that the main thing needful is to return to real

Christianity, apart from which all the plans and devices of the wisest will prove of little avail. . . . Never cease to urge upon men of every class, upon the highest placed as well as the lowly, the Gospel doctrines of Christian life." [*Condition of the Working Classes.*]

THE ECONOMICS OF NATIONALISM[1]

The science of Economics is commonly held to be lamentably arid and dismal. If that is your experience of it, blame the economists. For the slice of life, with which Economics has to deal, vibrates and, so to say, bleeds with human actuality. All science, all exploration, all history in its material factors, the whole epic of man's effort to subdue the earth and establish himself on it, fall within the domain of the economist. His material consists of the ordinary man in the ordinary business of mundane life, that, namely, of getting a living. This means more than food, clothes, and shelter. The highest activities of art and religion can function only under material forms. Churches have to be paid for as well as factories; you can no more get a bar of Caruso for nothing than you can get a bar of soap for nothing. Economics, moreover, is committed to an analysis not only of the production, but also of the distribution of wealth. In other words, it has to face formally the vast and dismaying problem of poverty. In the accomplishment of these tasks, moreover, the economist, preoccupied with one mode of organization among mankind, must necessarily consider the influence on it of other modes devised or evolved for other ends. Politics imposes itself on him. He can evade the political aspect of his material only by evading reality.

[1] Part of a paper read at St. Patrick's College, Maynooth, December 5, 1912.

THE DAY'S BURDEN

I

It is to a special hinterland of this last tract of territory that I wish to direct your minds to-night. Our inquiry is simple enough, and begins, as far as concerns myself, with a personal examination of conscience. Does the title National Economics amount to a contradiction in terms? If it does not, and if the nation holds a legitimate place in economc life and thought, is it that of a blessing or that of a nuisance? And if it is beneficient can we formulate an economic ideal fitted to express the self-realization of a nation which is resolute to realize itself?

A good many critics, endowed with that verbal deftness so characteristic of Irish critics, have said to me : " You have a Chair of National Economics in your college. Have you also by any chance a Chair of National Trigonometry or National Biology ? " The gibe does not go home. So long as you keep to the sphere of the highly abstract sciences any limiting particularity is certainly incongruous. But as you pass from the greyness of theory to the golden-green foliage of the tree of life, to the rich and endless differentiation of concrete fact, the incongruity diminishes. A National Mathematics is absurd ; a National Biology is not quite so absurd, seeing that every country has its own peculiar flora and fauna. When you come to a National Economics the incongruity has wholly disappeared. Plainly you can constitute for each nation under that title a branch of Descriptive Economics. Plainly since one nation is at one stage of growth, and another at another, and since the economy of each is, so to say, steeped and soaked in its temperament and history, your corpus of fact will in each case be strongly individual. Plainly you will have in each case a separate therapeutic. But I suggest to you that the doctrine of Nationalism in Economics goes far deeper than that.

Nationality is a principle of organization. You may regard it as ultimate and good, or as transitorial and bad, and there is no narrowly scientific test by which either view can be dismissed. But in accordance with your first standpoint your whole outlook is determined. Now, there is no doubt that the classical or English school of Political Economy did appear in its early years to be an almost irresistible solvent of Nationalism. You will find in Toynbee's *Industrial Revolution* two curiously similar judgments to that effect left on record by two such conflicting contemporaries as Coleridge and Napoleon. The reasons are in no way mysterious. The Classicists were all for freedom—free trade, free contract, free competition—and Nationalism appeared to them under the form of restrictions on freedom. Internal tolls were disappearing: why should not the custom-house disappear? Self-contained manor and self-contained town had been fused by a long historical process into the nation: why should not the nations be fused into a world-economy? The tides seemed to be setting in that direction. Capital was becoming at once more powerful and more fluid, and there is in capital an inherent cosmopolitanism. Labour moved towards internationalism as an essential part of its "gospel of deliverance." What were armies and navies but the watch-dogs of the rich? What were national flags and songs but parts of a ritual which they employed to intoxicate and exploit the poor? "The proletariat," cried out Marx in his thunderous manifesto, "has no fatherland." The whole thought of that period is, indeed, dyed in the grain with cosmopolitanism. And then there comes that sudden upheaving renaissance, and Nationalism is there as a colossal fact. The simplest account of the change is that it was a spontaneous outgush from the deep wells of human nature, and from the overlaid but unexhausted springs of history. From that time on to our own every nation sets deliberately about the task of self-realization, material and intellectual.

The English bias towards the "classical" economy was readily intelligible. Dominating the world she took her dominance for granted: she was unconscious of her nationality in the sense in which an entirely healthy man is unconscious of his digestion: and she devised a regime under which every other nation should be, in reference to her, a pupil and a tributary. But as the forces of growth matured and expanded in other nations they declined to Peter-Pan it to England. And so effective was their refusal that if you turn to a contemporary German text-book you will find the three periods of modern economic thought formally classified as (1) Mercantilism, (2) Liberalism, and (3) Nationalism.

What is the case for Nationalism? Well, if you turn to the leaders of the revolt of which I have spoken, such as List, or Henry Carey, the Irish-American, you will find a scientific or semi-scientific statement of it. If you turn to a modern leader of the revolt against what I may call Juggernaut Imperialism, such as Mr. Chesterton, you will find a better statement in terms of poetry and human nature. . . . You will, of course, bear in mind that Mr. Chesterton is not sufficiently dull to be authoritative. Being an artist, he is ever labouring to add to an old truth the radiance of a new beauty, which compromises him with the grave and the learned. . . . Let me try in a less adequate way to suggest in outline the creed of Nationalism. Professor Cannan, in his recent book, *The Economic Outlook*, elaborates an antithesis between Socialism and Nationalism. And in that form the case for Nationalism is best stated. His view would seem

to be not that Nationalism is visibly dying, but that
it can be shown to be obviously incompatible with
Socialism, and that, therefore, presumably, it must
die.

The stern, inevitable logic of this conclusion
escapes me. The presence of the steam engine on
George Stephenson's pioneer railway was incompatible with the presence of the cow, but it was not
the engine that perished in the encounter. The
whole tradition of Europe is for Nationalism and
against Socialism. Give us deep-cutting reforms;
liberate and redeem labour; bind property and
service in a bond that must be respected; assume
for the nation all the economic functions which in
the hands of individuals degenerate into waste or
tyranny; render it impossible for any man to
become, by mere dead weight of money, master of
his fellows, body and soul. So far we are with you.
But propose to ladle us all, with all that we own
and are, into your communistic hotch-pot, and,
entrenched behind the ancient bulwarks of personality, family, nationality, we repel and annihilate
you in the name of civilization. If too much
unearned property is the grave of freedom, some
earned property, with the seal of service on it, is
the cradle of freedom. Even in Ibsen the button-
moulder was able to fling back Peer Gynt into the
melting-pot only because Peer had remained all his
life a mere self-amorous incoherence, in the true
sense, a nonentity. But the nation that is a richly
positive entity cannot so be dissolved and dismissed.
Destroy Nationalism, and you extinguish the sacrificial flames about which the greatest nobleness of
the world has gathered in abnegation. You shatter
the altar vessels in which the precious wine of
freedom has been passed from lip to lip.

" Cosmopolitanism," says Turgénev in *Rudin*, " is
all twaddle. . . . Even the ideal face must have

an individual expression." This humanity, to the
worship of which you are to butcher Nationalism,
is too vast, too vague, too bloodless an abstraction.
Our arms are not long enough to fold it in an
embrace. Ireland I feel equal to, and Dublin, and
that windy Atlantic cliff, straining out against the
ocean and the sunset, and that farmer to whom I
spoke at Tralee fair, and that publican in Tyrone,
and the labourers, spoiled by unemployment, who
come to me at my house nearly every day, and for
whom I can get no work. But as for the world as
a whole, even its geography is too large for my head,
to say nothing of its problems, and its emotions are
too large for my heart. What is humanity? You
and I and the man round the corner, or over the sea,
are humanity. And if it is the nature of us all to
come to amplest self-expression by living our lives
here and now, for a community which is small
enough to know and to love, then by "transcending"
national categories you do not enrich, you impover-
ish, humanity.

Nationalism, indeed, like every other fine faith,
has the misfortune to be judged less by its core of
dogma than by its shell of superstition. Tariffism
and militarism are its apes, not the authentic sons
of its house. The parallel to which appeal has been
made avails here also. If I knock you down in the
street, or, when you call on me, slam the door in
your face, these are beyond all doubt impressive
proofs of the fact that I enjoy an existence separate
from yours. But there are other and better proofs,
as, for instance, to buy from you, to learn from you,
to feed, foster, or help you. There are better ways
of putting heads together than banging them
together. In precisely the same way a nation
degrades and cancels Nationalism by choosing to
identify it with isolation or aggressiveness. The
first blunder is at war with the conscience of all

ages: a character as Goethe says, can fashion itself only in the stream of the world. The second is certainly at war with the conscience of this age. To receive hospitably, and assimilate deeply; to toil, to think, and to communicate without penury or reserve—these remain the marks of a strong nation as of a strong man. Free trade in ideas as in commodities is the desired regime of those who have attained maturity. But it is a strange altruism which bids me not only give myself, but slay myself, so that at the end of the process there is no basis left either for self-regarding or for altruistic action. I must own myself in order to give myself.

Curiously enough, it is in the writings of contemporary theorists of continental Socialism that we find the most eloquent repudiation of Professor Cannan's philosophy. Practice had preceded theory. Labour once thought—in the days of the *Communist Manifesto*—that its destiny centered in cosmopolitanism. On that basis it sought to construct an International, but it failed, and the failure led to a notable transformation of Marxism. To-day you have an International that possesses reality because it roots in Nationalism. We Nationalists may appeal to the authoritative words of Professor Sombart in his *Socialism and the Social Movement* :—

" Marx's opinion, ' The working-classes have no fatherland,' is being replaced by another, ' If that is so, let us give them one.' . . . The view is gaining ground among Socialists—indeed especially among them—that all civilization has its roots in nationality, and that civilization can reach its highest development only on the basis of nationality."

He goes on to quote glowing and splendid passages from David and Penestorfer, to one of which we may appeal :

"Socialism and national idea are thus not opposed to each other; they rather supplement each other. Every attempt to weaken the national idea is an attempt to lessen the precious possessions of mankind. . . . Socialism wants to organize, and not disintegrate, humanity. But in the organisms of mankind, not individuals, but nations, are the tissues, and if the whole organism is to remain wholly healthy, it is necessary for the tissues to be healthy."

As for your capitalist who, in those days, was a cosmopolitan, he is now in every country a jingo. Herr Goldenberg is no sooner settled in Park Lane than you find his name heading the list of subscriptions to Lord Roberts' Conscription League.

The general significance of the new politics is twofold. It substitutes an organic for the old atomistic conception of economic life. And in establishing the nation as a principle of organization it establishes it also as a principle of sacrifice, and therein provides the only basis of Protection that is not intellectually disreputable.

II

Such "sentimentalities" will strike strangely and even harshly on the ears of those who have been bred up to believe that Political Economy began with Adam Smith and ended with John Stuart Mill, and that between 1780 and 1850 the laws underlying the business life of mankind were defined, once and for all, in immutable formulæ. The line of thought suggested by them is very ill represented in English text-books. There is a reason for the lacuna, as for most things, and it lies on the surface. If you want a full appreciation of the significance of health you must go not to the athlete's gymnasium, but to the hospital ward. If you want an appreciation of the value of national freedom and unity, you must go, not to the one nation which entered the Steam Age with these foundations of greatness deeply established, but to one of those which, during the nineteenth century, had to work out their salvation, political and economic, through blood and tears. During the period of crystallization of the Classical Economy the industrial hegemony of Great Britain was absolute. Her supremacy in coal, in iron, in shipping, in machinery, in the technique of manufacture was unchallenged. On this basis the great theorists, like Ricardo, implicitly, if not deliberately, proceeded. The system which they evolved was at once too English in matter, too abstract in method, and too dogmatic in tone. Protests against its exclusiveness, its insularity, could be multiplied from the pages of Continental economics. Thus Adolph Wagner, the great Austrian master, summarizing Roscher, a precursor, in his *Foundations*, writes:—

"They (the English school) have a tendency to rely solely on abstract deduction, and to exaggerate its importance . . . .; in theory, but especially in practice, they isolate economic phenomena too radically from the other social phenomena with which they are intimately associated; they assign to economic phenomena and institutions, and to their solutions of economic questions, a character too absolute, instead of assigning only that relative and historical character which is proper to all the facts of history; their verdict on Free Trade, and its results, is in many respects erroneous, and a great deal too optimistic; they efface the State too completely, and misunderstand its rôle as regulator of the national economy."

This judgment, which is not precisely a con-
demnation of scientific principles, but rather a
methodological admonition, may now be said to be
universally accepted. It is interesting to note that
one of the first, and most influential, writers to
propagate it in English was John Kells Ingram.
Still more interesting is it to note the essential
identity of the human reality behind it with that
behind "Who Fears to Speak of '98?" The red fire
of passion has been transmuted into the illumination
of science, but here, as always, Ingram voices the
revolt of the small nations against the Czarism,
scientific and political, of the great. The reaction
in Economics is most adequately represented by the
German Historical School. Of its leaders, from List
and Roscher to Schmoller and Wagner, it is not
too much to say that every nerve and fibre of their
science quivers with Nationalism. The simplest
account of German history during the second generation of the nineteenth century is that it was the
adolescence of a giant. It is significant of the giant's
future that, during that period, he finds it most
natural to call the study of business life not "Political
Economy" or merely "Economics," but "National
Economics," *Nationaloekonomik*. From the purely
scientific point of view the reaction was, undoubtedly,
carried too far. If it was the fashion of the Classical
School to dogmatize about everything, from a
minimum of experience, it became that of the
Historical School to accumulate all the experience
of all time, and then to decline to dogmatize about
anything. The one sect burned incense, and very
often offered up human sacrifice, on the altar of
inexorable laws. The other did, indeed, question
from time to time the propriety of certain details of
the ritual, but their dissent went very much deeper.
They said simply: There are no such laws. You
are worshipping the non-existent. But as spokes-

men of real life against the phantasm of the intellect,
which had come to be mistaken for real life, the
historical economists were wholly in the right. The
fruitfulness of their influences is best witnessed by
a writer who does not wholly sympathize with it.
Thus Professor Landry, one of the leaders of the
newer generation in France, observes in his *Manuel
d'Economique* :—

"It is much easier now to distinguish the
Economics of one nation from that of another
than it was at the beginning of the nineteenth
century. This results in part from the fact that
in the interval the content of Economics has been
greatly enriched, and, in consequence, greatly
diversified. But it is also to be explained by the
development, during the nineteenth century, of
the spirit of Nationalism in, at all events, many
parts of the civilized world. For more than a
hundred years the countries in question have
deliberately sought to differentiate themselves in
the region of scientific research from their neighbours. Indeed, strange and deplorable as it may
seem, there are even countries in which economic
writers deliberately cover with contempt the productive economy of their neighbours, or else
refuse to consider it at all."

That the Historical School should also be, under
another aspect, the National School, can occasion
no surprise. On the one hand, if you turn to history
at all the first fact that impresses itself is the colossal
fact of nationality : on the other, every concrete
nationality is in origin, form and tendency an historical product.

So much for what we may style the rehabilitation
of the national idea. I may seem to you to have
laboured it too much with something of a Falstaffian

parade of erudition : if so, the explanation is obvious. When you come to mix in the actual life of our contemporary Ireland, you will find everybody on the one side concerned about national self-realization, political and economic. You will find everybody on the other parrotting forth the perennial nonsense that the Irish question is not political but purely economic. You will turn to some standard text-book for enlightenment—in the nature of things it will be an English text-book—and you will be confused and discouraged to find principles, which you greatly value, either cheapened or ignored. I have tried to suggest to you that there is an historical explanation for all this. Continental experience comes much closer to ours than does English experience, and Continental thought, is, as a result, a much truer source of guidance. To offer a purely economic solution for a politico-economic problem, such as ours, is futile, and even absurd. It is as if a doctor were to tell his patient, that once his lungs are brought back to health, it does not matter whether there is an aneurism in his heart or not.

It should be added that the line of criticism suggested is fully valid only as against the popularizers, not as against the masters of the English school.

III

The acceptance of the national as against the individual, of the organic as against the atomistic, point of view, transforms nearly every economic problem. Let us consider one or two of them very briefly, and first of all that of external trade policy.

I have already described what may be called platform Protectionism as intellectually disreputable. The orthodox Free Trader has no difficulty in riddling it. It is true that, theoretically in certain posited conditions, and in one or two rare instances in practice, a tax on an import may be thrown back on to the foreign producer. But, in general, the very object of a Protective tariff is to raise prices, obtainable by the home producer, and payable by the home consumer, in the home market. If that object is not attained the tariff affords no " Protection." In the long run the increase of prices may, indeed, lead to the exploitation of native resources, hitherto untapped, and prices may gradually sink to their former level. But, for the time being, a tribute is, and must be, levied on the consumer. How, then, are we to describe except as impostors the Protectionists who run gaily about the country with their big and their little loaves, and all the rest of the paraphernalia, explaining that they are going to make everybody richer by adding a tax to the price of everything ? So far, the Manchester stalwart is certainly entitled to the verdict as against him of Birmingham. But, when we have reached this point, the controversy is so far from being at an end that it is in truth only beginning. The advocate of taxed, as against untaxed, imports retreats to higher ground, or rather launches his charge from it. We have already quoted one great Irishman, Dr. Ingram; we now fall back on another, Professor Bastable, both of Trinity College, Dublin :—

" To understand the position taken up by the modern opponents of Free Trade (writes Professor Bastable in his *Commerce of Nations*), it is, above all, essential to recognize that the key-note of their system is nationality. . . . The claims of the nation as a whole are accentuated, and regarded as far more important than those of the individual, or the world at large."

The nation has a continuity of existence to which

141

none of its children can pretend. It has been from of old; it will still be long after the dust of this generation has been blown about the barren plains, or sealed within the iron hills. Given such an organism, so extended in space and time, it is reasonable to sacrifice the welfare of a part of it to that of the whole, and to sacrifice its own present to its future. The nation is held to be entitled to require from each of its citizens, even in time of peace, tax-contributions which will be spent on great public objects in which assuredly he has no bread-and-butter interest; in time of war, it will exact from him his property, his service in arms, and finally his blood. The nation does not live by bread alone, but, if its bread fails, the special type of culture of which it is the representative must perish. Is it not clear, then, that if the industrial and cultural strength of a people is compromised by the trend of its trade, the government of that people has the right to interfere, to impose minor economic sacrifices on this or that class, for the behoof of the community, and even to lay burdens on the whole community for the benefit of its future citizens in the same spirit in which a father will work hard, and live sparely, in order to secure for his children a place in the sun?

Such circumstances may be held to exist in three typical situations:—

(1) If the effect of foreign importation is to confine, or depress, to low-grade industries a country capable of high-grade industries.

(2) If a country is known to possess great industrial possibilities which have, nevertheless, been over-laid and annulled by the disastrous accidents of history, and by the inertia which has thus been engendered.

(3) If the development of a country has been one-sided—a predominance, let us say, of manu-

facture over agriculture—so as to leave it dependent on the ends of the earth for its food-supply, and so to increase enormously the perils of war.

In such instances it may be argued that the levy imposed on the consumer by a customs tariff is analogous to public expenditure on education, or on defence. I am not—let me observe—making out a case for Protection, but merely indicating a plane upon which there may be made out a case which, although it may be fallacious, is certainly very far from being a mere imposture. You will notice that the central reality from which all these arguments, economic and non-economic, radiate, the dogma which lends them their whole value and vitality, is that of sacrifice, temporary or permanent, in the name of Nationalism.

It would be misleading not to add that, on the same plane and in terms of the same creed, a policy of Free Trade, not merely for the England, but for the Ireland of 1913, may be vindicated. Here, again, the national interest, and not the interest of this or that individual, is paramount. The reply runs:—

(1) Protective duties, being a mode of indirect taxation, oppress the poor, to the advantage of the rich, and so poison the wells of national renewal.

(2) They do not evoke efficiency, but merely shelter and stereotype inefficiency.

(3) They lead to profound corruption of the national political life.

(4) If we are to subsidize experimental industries, let it be done openly through the medium of bounties or grants definitely assigned to the promoters of such enterprises to enable them to train labour.

I am myself a Free Trader, varying from the orthodox, United Kingdom type, however, in laying strong emphasis on this last rubric. That this is my view is not a matter of much importance. But it is a matter of considerable importance that it was the view of John Stuart Mill. It may, or may not, be known to those who are so fond of his "infant industries" exception, but it is a fact that he withdrew from the position taken up in that passage. Actual observation of the pernicious effects on public life of tariff experiments in the Australian colonies, and in America, led to that withdrawal :—

"I am now (he writes, in 1868) much shaken in the opinion, which has so often been quoted for purposes which it did not warrant; and I am disposed to think that when it is advisable, as it may sometimes be, to subsidize a new industry in its commencement, this had better be done by a direct annual grant, which is far less likely to be continued after the conditions which alone justified it have ceased to exist."

So much for external trade policy. Let us now turn to certain matters of internal development, bearing in mind always that we are not attempting to examine them fully on their merits, but only to construe them in terms of Economic Nationalism. The struggle in Ireland between pasture and tillage and the future of our railway system will serve as examples.

Nothing has so much compromised economic science in this country as the fact that "the Economists" were supposed to have approved of all the clearances and consolidations which came from 1820 on, and to have greeted the cattle-jobbing grazier with a pæan of applause as the first true specimen of the *homo œconomicus* vouchsafed to

Ireland. In Sir Samuel Ferguson's remarkable poem, "Inheritor and Economist," the reader will find them denounced with extraordinary vehemence on these and other scores. And the pity is that although very ill-founded as affecting a great Liberal like Mill, they were very well-founded as affecting the journalistic popularizers. When *The Times* wrote that in Ireland "man had for long been a nuisance, and population a drug on the market," that diagnosis was eminently orthodox. Ireland, to the popularizers, was an entirely simple case of over-population. Since any one part of the earth was, to their cosmopolitanism, very much the same as any other—England and her chosen people always, of course, implicitly excepted—and since it was the nature of labour and of capital to flow to the point of maximum productiveness, the emigration of men and money was a normal, and even a beneficent, phenomenon. Indeed, M'Culloch went very near saying that the drain of absentee rents was a positive advantage. Moreover, with that extravagant optimism for which Wagner rebukes them, he and his friends never wavered in their faith that the line of maximum personal acquisitiveness is also the line of maximum public benefit. And so, beyond doubt, the gambler in cattle entered the rural economy of Ireland, panoplied in the "Laws of Political Economy." Indeed, so long as we keep to the individual as against the national, to the atomistic as against the organic conception of economic life, the ranches are unassailable. It would be difficult to cite many instances in which the quotient $\frac{\text{net personal profit}}{\text{personal effort}}$ is not as large, or very nearly as large, for the grass-farmer as it would be for the holder of an equal extent of land devoted to mixed farming. It is to be remembered that, in the former case, effort is reduced to a minimum,

L 145

and leisure raised to a maximum. But the moment we apply the touchstone of national interest the whole aspect of the problem alters. Mixed farming will give an indefinitely larger gross output, and support a correspondingly larger number of people. Not only will it enrich the nation in point of numbers, but it will, by the greater variety and difficulty of its technique, improve them in intellectual and moral quality.

Appeal to the gospel of Economic Nationalism, and the controversy is closed: reject that gospel, fall back on what are, rather ridiculously, styled "purely business considerations," and there is no reason why your *latifundia* should not increase instead of disappearing.

The railway system you can similarly regard, either as a profit-earning enterprise for certain individuals, or as a fundamental instrument of national development. If you take the former view, the line of exploitation of these railways ought to be simply that of maximum dividends. You may argue, if you like, that this will also be the line of maximum public advantage, but, unless you have a singular aptitude for rose-coloured visions, you will find it hard to convince even yourself of the truth of this proposition. Take the other point of view, and it becomes your duty so to use the railways as to maximise national production. You are entitled to act on long-run instead of short-run calculations; to lose money, for the time being, instead of making money; to undertake, for the sake of the future, large expenditures by way of subsidy and re-organization which, under private enterprise, would be either impossible or else a fraud on your shareholders.

These illustrations might be almost indefinitely multiplied. But this paper has already run to inordinate length, and I must close it, leaving unanswered my own question as to the economic ideal which Ireland ought to set before herself. That must stand over for some other occasion. Had there been time to consider it, much of our discussion must have turned on the country town. That, and not the great city, is the germinal cell of industrial expansion in Ireland. In function as in name it is capable of effecting a synthesis of our two great interests, falsely supposed to be irreconcilable enemies. The country town must manufacture or perish. As capital accumulates in the hands of the new farmers, our condition of progress will be realized. As soon as they come to understand that the safest investment for it is not some oil or rubber mirage in the waste of the earth but an enterprise, associated with farming, conducted under their own eyes and their own control, the economy of Ireland will be transformed.

That is a mere suggestion. For the moment, I must be content with having unfolded to you the outline of an argument which re-establishes Nationalism, and national self-direction, as ranking among the human First Principles of material prosperity. If it helps you to join up the dreams—as yet unformulated—of the Irish nation with the intellectual tradition of Europe, then I shall not have wasted either your evening or my own.

LABOUR : WAR OR PEACE

Our contemporary world is modestly conscious of
the possession of many qualities the excellence or
the reality of which it would be idle to deny; we
have curiosity, spaciousness of vision, and a very
notable turn for the exposition of depressing truths.
But we have our defects, and one of them stands
nakedly out like a headland; we may not be more
frightened than our forerunners, but we are frightened
on a larger scale. We have the genius of panic.
Every difficulty, caught up into the enlarging
atmosphere of our newspapers, becomes forthwith a
crisis, every trouble a tragedy, every political blunder
a planned betrayal of the nation and posterity. There
is not a school-child in the land but has already
survived at least three or four final cataclysms, and
ends-of-all-things. We must not seem to suggest
that this faculty of exaggeration is characteristically
modern, it is as old as the hills and human nature.
The world over, and at all periods, the worst evil to
any man is that which at the moment has him in its
claws. Last year's influenza is tolerable in comparison with this year's cold; a boot, which pinches
me here and now, nips out of my consciousness all
the fantastic tortures of China. And if there is any
sphere in which even a slight jolt to the established
order may naturally and almost reasonably set us
alarming one another it is certainly that of industry.
The economic process is one from which none of us
can stand apart, unless we chance to be at one and
the same time rich and mad. For the ninety per
cent. of us for whom ninety per cent. of the energy
of daily life is committed to the conquest of bread

the movements of economic life have all the fascination of a great machine, imperfectly understood,
indispensable, and full of menace. Every new
development seems to make it more subtle and, by
consequence, more vulnerable. The old stable
societies, we say to ourselves, were a Temple of
Gaza, they might crash down in ruins, but at least
one saw the vast arms of Samson knotted about
the pillars before the crash. In our new society with
its amazing network of international trade, finance,
science, and anarchism, there need be no such great
and visible intervention. Let somebody only push
a lever, or even press an electric button, out of
season, or, still worse, decline to push or press them
and the whole fabric falls to pieces. And here, we
go on, you have the only people who know how to
work the most essential parts of the complication
perpetually grumbling, with perpetual threats. Is
it not the end of all things, or something very like
it? With what assurance can we keep on believing
that the world will last our time? In the improbable
contingency of any world continuing to exist it will
certainly not be that which has so far nourished us,
and our achievements. It will be, on the contrary,
a sort of blood-stained Bedlam, the plans of which
have already been prepared by a number of unpro-
nounceable foreign, and unspeakable home agitators,
hideously devoted to the hideous cult of Syndicalism.

   This picture exaggerates no doubt, but not greatly,
the exaggerations of our modern fear. But it is a
recognizable transcript of the talk of the railway
train, the club smoke-room, and the golf-links, that
is to say of the three foci of middle-class civilization.
Such an attitude of mind is, in many respects, a
public gain of extreme importance. It has at least
broken up the monstrous apathy of the comfortable,
and delivered them from the sin of being at ease in
Zion. It may save them from that, as imaginative

persons are sometimes saved from drink by the sight of twisted, sinister, and non-existent snakes. But such terror is not a good foundation for a sound economic system, nor, on reflection, will it bear the scrutiny of recent experience. Transportation and fuel are fundamental necessities, but neither the railwaymen's strike, nor the miners' strike, nor, for that matter, any other of the late industrial disturbances affords any justification for the despair which it is now fashionable to affect. The world has known, and lived through, much dirtier weather. No man of prudent temper will seek to underrate the gravity of these conflicts. But there were brave men before Achilles, and there were strikes before those strikes. They are to be regarded as no more than incidents in the epic of labour, and in the large epic of humanity ; they spring from old and familiar causes ; and in the real and vital forces, which function behind them, there is nothing that threatens a new dispensation. There is a test at hand which hardly anybody ever dreams of applying. The reader is invited to forget, for the moment, what he reads about the dismal procession of life, and to recall what he sees, and his own rôle as a marcher in it. If he encounters, day by day, red ruin and the breaking up of laws, pale riders on white horses, and apocalyptic dawns, no more is to be said. He belongs to the "intellectual minority," the "remnant," and those of us who do not may wish him joy of his ticket of admission. With us modern life has not yet dealt so harshly. We have not been menaced in our morning bath by any Charlotte Corday of domestic Syndicalism, or bidden by the porter at our suburban station to off coat and shovel coal, or by the newsboy to plunge into the brattle of the composing-room. We find that meat, milk, clothes, transportation, and even an accurate report of Professor Schafer, are still to be had in exchange for the very different services which, as the outcome of a series of accidents, we happen to be at present rendering to society. Looking out we discover the way of the world to be, in view of all the prophecies, scandalously familiar. People in general are observed to be still enduring the ancient discipline, and exploiting the ancient joys of life. Dedicated to plough, loom, and engine they still seem to keep on grumbling and toiling ; making little of much and much of little ; homely, loyal, industrious, reckless, impatient ; interested in religion, happiness, the prospects of the football season and the Insurance Act. Some of them even reach as high as the crucial Act of Hope ; they marry and desire children.

So much is necessary by way of striking the key in which any useful discussion of our present industrial inconveniences must proceed. Mr. Wells lately announced that until we became conscious that everything touching labour is new—a new atmosphere, a new mood, a new outlook—we must abide blind and impotent. The truth is that, viewed in another aspect, everything is as old as the edict that joined bread with the sweat of a man's brow, and that, although the colour of the counters may change, the game in its essentials does not change. The answer, the simple and the sole adequate answer, to Socialism, to Syndicalism, to every perversion is human nature. But the key thus set, every honest inquirer will admit that we are in presence of a serious situation, not at all novel, and not so menacing as the wolf-shouters are pleased to think, but, for all that, exacting and doubtful. People ask indignantly: Why is Labour discontented? But how could it be anything else? The condition of the workers of these islands is not such as either to command or deserve permanence. Thirty per cent. of them, more than twelve million human beings, count themselves fortunate if they are able to hold their places in the dim borderland where destitution merges into mere poverty. They are constantly slipping into the blacker depths, sometimes to recover their hold, sometimes to perish. As we go higher in the hierarchy of skill and opportunity, things, no doubt, improve, but we have to go unexpectedly and painfully high before we reach the plane of the genuine living wage. And once on that plane, or nearing it, a new force comes into play. We are caught in the sweep of the law of economic progress, the simplest statement of which is that, having put an inch between himself and destitution, a man will seek to put an ell. The sublimical worker, if one may so call him, is numbed by the weight on him, without hope and in the end almost without feeling. Ease the pressure, and the forces of growth are released in his soul. He advances in education that is to say, he advances at once in sensitiveness, in economic appetite, and in power of organization. Something will have much, and much will have more. In his vision the future, whether construed in personal or in social terms, must be progressively better than the past. Too often he produces his line of desire to infinity, quits altogether the sober and fettered earth, and loses himself in the millennial mirage of Socialism. Now it is submitted that you have here, in all essential features, the story of what has been called the epic of labour. The strike, now and then intensifies some episode of it into drama, but the pull of the deep under-currents is always at work. Those of us who believe individualism to be the ultimate and permanent form of any free society, are a shade too fond of lecturing labour. There is no use in lecturing labour, we had better understand it. Let us, therefore, say frankly that the condition of our poorest is a poignant and horrible fact. It does not justify the enfeebling sentimentality or the blood-hunger of what a speaker at the Trade Union

LABOUR: WAR OR PEACE?

Congress described the other day as the "flapdoodle revolutionaries." But it is an urgent and ever-present warning to us that, while we defend and conserve our present industrial fabric on its fundamental lines, we must drastically re-model many of its subsidiary features. Moreover, we had better recognize that if the desire of labour to make its future better than its past is criminal, then we are all tarred with the same guilty brush. The continuity of family life, and wise instinct which sets men planting acorns so that their children may enjoy the matured oak, are the best economic bulwarks of the institution of private property. If anybody is to have the inspiration of this hope then everybody must have it. With greater justice it might be complained that the rising standard of life among the workers tends in some respects, in the direction of mere waste and luxury. But who can appear in court sufficiently clean-handed to lodge that complaint? If the "lower classes" are corrupted it is the "middle" and "upper" classes that have been their educators in corruption; it does not lie with these latter to preach any very honest asceticism. The truth is that if you look at humanity in the mass you will find it not much worse and not much better than its familiar, historical record. Desire still keeps it on the march, and desire in all sorts and conditions of men occasionally puffs itself out into an intolerable egotism and lust for luxury. But if you examine the form which it takes among the mass of industrial labourers in our day, you will find it to be modest in the extreme. A little more leisure, a little more comfort, a little more security of life, some slight treasure of hope to bequeath to one's children.

So much for what may be taken to be the all but universal psychology of labour unrest. Is there any ground for believing that recent manifestations have transformed an old problem, integrally and beyond recognition? To the present writer it seems that there is none, or, at most, very little, and that very vague. He submits the following analysis of the situation.

The late strikes were not serious beyond precedent.

It is not necessary to involve any panic-stricken hypothesis of a new Anarchism in order to explain them; they can be traced, in great part, to certain objective and, so to say, mechanical conditions.

The " New Anarchism " is neither so new in idea, nor so minatory in fact, as is supposed. Nevertheless, society is in an unstable equilibrium, and the time is ripe for a reconsideration of the whole wage-system, and of every device by which its harshness and variability may be mitigated.

The first of these statements speaks but too plainly for itself. It is not necessary to go back to the Peasants' Revolt, or the *tire de Lyon*, or to the blind Samson smashing machines and getting himself ridden down by cavalry at Peterloo, of the hangings and transportations of the strikers of the eighteen-forties, or to the Irish Land War, in order to find parallels. The single point of interest in such an historical retrospect is that any of these disturbances of the established order is now seen to have been more humane and tolerable than the order which it disturbed. But in modern industry, and in our own time, the strike has been rather a normal feature than a deplorable extravaganza. For the decade 1901-10 the figures for Great Britain and Ireland show an annual average of 464 trade disputes, affecting 221,059 workers, and involving the loss yearly of 4,260,859 days. If we extend the period, and bring in France (which, it is well to remember, was in this regard not the corrupter but the pupil of England), we arrive at the following table :

WORKING DAYS LOST THROUGH TRADE DISPUTES

	United Kingdom	France
1891—1895	14,032,298	1,497,768
1896—1900	7,010,096	1,990,546
1901—1905	2,791,257	3,228,490
1906—1908	5,947,000	4,907,000

For 1911 the United Kingdom statistics record 864 trade disputes, affecting 931,050 workers, and involving the loss of 10,247,100 working days. This is a lamentable increase, but if we recover perspective by putting it into comparison with other great strike years, it does not seem so overwhelming:

WORKING DAYS LOST THROUGH TRADE DISPUTES
IN THE UNITED KINGDOM

1893	31,205,062
1897	11,463,523
1898	14,171,478
1908	10,834,188
1911	10,247,100

The figures for the first six months of 1912 are, indeed, dismaying. In that period no fewer than 37,500,000 working days were lost through trade disputes, notably that of March. But large as that number is it does not constitute a phenomenon of a new order. Those cited serve to show that there are but too many melancholy precedents for our unrest. Nor do available records bear out what we may call the bound-to-be-beaten argument so often addressed to strikers. The following table summarizes, by percentages, for the period 1900-1909, the results of the strikes which took place in five great industrial countries in Europe:

1900-1909

All Strikes	Country	Victory complete or partial of strikers	Defeat of Strikers
100	Belgium	34·89	65·11
100	Germany	54·21	45·79
100	United Kingdom	56·44	43·56
100	France	64·19	35·81
100	Italy	66·60	33·40

It is to be borne in mind that these percentages are calculated in terms of the number of strikes, and do not give an accurate picture of the magnitude of the interests affected. But we have the definite testimony of the railway leaders that their strike "paid," as they say, "a substantial dividend," and the same holds, beyond doubt, of the miners. The strike, therefore, would appear to be by no means the abnormal and by no means the discredited manœuvre which it is, in some quarters, supposed to be.

But it is said that the late employment of it on a large scale is a phenomenon of a new order, because it was deliberately motived by the new policy of Syndicalism. The argument apparently is that if M. Georges Sorel had never written his *Reflections on Violence*, the miners would never have struck for a minimum wage, and Mr. Ben Tillett would never have had occasion to pray for Lord Devonport. So stated, the attempt to ascribe—whether by way of boastfulness or of terror—all contemporary labour troubles to the malign impulse of Syndicalism wears its unreality on its face. There is no need to soar to any such abstract and refined theory. A single, hard concrete fact is sufficient to explain the restiveness of labour, the divergence, namely, between the standard of money wages and the cost of living. To raise the former a little above the latter is, when

all is said and done, the main effort of organized
labour, and we are accustomed to acclaim, if not
the whole of the nineteenth century, at all events
the Victorian Age as having been, in that regard, a
period of growing success. The year 1850 or there-
abouts had come to be regarded as the turning of
the tide. Without striking into a maze of statistics
we may summarize the general significance for labour
of the period in two passages from two great economists, Thorold Rogers writing in England and
Professor Gide in France. Having characterized
the earlier centuries of which we possess records,
Rogers goes on :

". . . . in the first half of the eighteenth
century, though still far below the level of the
fifteenth, it (the condition of the English labourer)
achieved comparative plenty. Then it began to
sink again, and the workman experienced the
direst misery during the great continental war.
Latterly, almost within our own memory and
knowledge, it has experienced a slow and partial
improvement, the causes of which are to be found
in the liberation of industry from protective laws,
in the adoption of certain principles which
restrained employment in some directions, and
most of all in the concession to labourers of the
right so long denied of forming labour partner-
ships."

Rogers had in mind mainly the first half of the
nineteenth century. Gide, with the complete picture
of it before him, echoes the same highly ambiguous
optimism. Judging by present experience, he
observes, the condition of the workers between 1800
and 1830 was "probably worse than at any previous
period in their history, very much worse than that
of preceding centuries." It was a "lugubrious age."

When the tide turned the inflow was tardy and penurious.

"If wages rose enormously during the last three-quarters of the nineteenth century we must, nevertheless, be on our guard against the illusion that they have even now reached a high level. What the movement means is that they started from a very low level. He may well be amazed at the fact that it took a hundred long years of conflict and advance to raise the wage of labour to the miserable figure at which, for the greater of the working class, it now stands."[1]

Thus testified Gide in 1900. In the intervening decade things have not bettered, but worsened. The curve of prices has outdistanced the curve of wages. The majority of economists appear to be agreed that this rise in prices, and especially in export prices, is due to the enormous increase in the output of gold. A similar upward jump between 1854 and 1863 is so to be explained. This upclimb of prices is held to have stimulated production, and even to have begotten a boom. But it has reacted sorely on labour. Professor Ashley estimates that a worker could buy as much for 20s. in 1896 as he could buy for about 24s. in 1910. Between these dates the price of food had risen, according to his estimate, by at least 19 per cent., according to that of Professor Gide by 25 per cent. Wages are calculated to have increased in the same period by not more than 11 per cent. These figures are, of course, largely conjectural, no complete inquiry having yet been made, but in so far as they are our daily experience must convince us that they err on the side of optimism. Such circumstances must inevitably produce unrest. The enormous economic pressure indicated has come

[1] *Institutions de Progrès Social.* **New Edition.** 1912.

most heavily, not on the budget which at all times has ample reserves, but on the line-ball budget of the wage-earner. The weakest feels it worst. The movement in prices has not merely checked the rising curve of working-class prosperity, but seems to have actually depressed it below its former level. In the opinion of Professor Ashley it has deprived labour "of all, and perhaps more than all," that it had gained in the way of higher wages in the last decade and a half.

This harsh and embittering experience would offer a sufficient explanation of more than the present discontent. That the discontent in question springs from defeat in the old struggle for food, shelter and clothes, and not from any new diabolism, is strikingly confirmed by Mr. Vernon Hartshorn, the ablest of the "revolutionaries." "This is not a question," he writes, "of Socialism or Syndicalism. . . . The worker is not out for a theory. He is out for something more tangible—bread."

But it is entirely natural that in such an atmosphere novel and violent doctrines should find audience if not acceptance. The ear of hunger is ready to listen to any new analysis of society, any new programme or campaign that announces itself in fervent and sweeping formulæ. In this case it is invited to a somewhat ragged version of the words of M. Sorel, and the deeds of M. Pataud. The poorness of the lodgment found by that version is obvious. At the recent Trade Union Congress there was to have been a full-dress debate on Syndicalism. All the heavy artillery was to have taken the field. But as it turned out there were but two delegates, two young Welsh miners, who attempted to defend the new creed, and neither of them was at any particular pains to define it. The Congress carried by a majority so large as to constitute an all but unanimous decision, an anti-Syndicalist resolution.

What the precise tenets of Syndicalism are it is far
from easy to say. This is claimed as a virtue, for it
is argued that vagueness and vitality go together.
"Why should you be expected," asks Mr. J. H.
Harley—in what we may call a tongue-in-the-cheek
exposition of Sorel—"to know the site of every
temple erected on the site of your expected New
Jerusalem. . . . Intellect is discursive and limitative;
it is intuition that gives us the rounded or perfect
whole." M. Bergson has said so, and the mantle of
his philosophy is deemed sufficient to cover a whole
mob of doctrines that would otherwise incur
suspicion. If vagueness is characteristic of the vital
impulse so also is violence, and the blinder it is the
better. This economic Agnosticism has its notable
advantages, but it may help also to explain the
Syndicalist revolt against Parliamentary government.
Parliamentarianism means elections, and elections
mean definite programmes. The election address of
a devotee of these doctrines would afford agreeable
reading:

"You ask me, comrade, whether I am in favour
of this, or in favour of that. In putting such a
question you are seeking to envelop my spontaneity
in the limitative, discursive, and generally low-
caste categories of intellect. Rise to the plane of
intuition on which alone a philosopher can consent
to dwell. My programme is this. I will Intuit.
I will creatively evolve. I will continually and
progressively sprout into fresh spontaneities. . . ."

It is to be feared that at this point some member
of the audience might be moved to intone the
popular American song: "I don't know where I'm
going, but I'm on my way." Nobody demands a
minute and accurately starred Baedeker of these
Utopians. The *lendemain de la Révolution* may well

be rather clouded and dim of prospect. But we are certainly entitled to demand something a little more or less definite. Fortunately many of the Syndicalists have so far forgotten themselves as to say what they mean. They offer apparently two contributions, one of which belongs to the practical and the other to the theoretical order. They have a recipe by which labour is to become master of the world, and a plan on which the world is to be reorganized after that mastery has been achieved. Let us take this latter first. It is proposed to replace the wage-system, by hypothesis overthrown, by a network of productive groups: in some schemes each of these groups is to own the instruments of production in its particular industry, in others the group is merely to control the techinque of production. In this second plan all industrial ownership is concentrated in the State, which also directs the whole process of distribution. It is difficult to discern any impressive novelty in this proposal. One form of it is merely a specialization and elaboration of socialism, and is steeped in all the injustices and impossibilities of that system. The other is a mere reproduction of the dreams of speculative Anarchists like Kropotkin—the free association of self-organized economic groups displacing that compulsory association which we call the State—and although conserving some sort of freedom it throws to the winds an element of co-equal importance, order. Both display, on examination, the lineaments of old friends, or rather, old enemies. They are the eternally repelled, eternally reappearing standards of decivilization. M. Sorel and his fellow-theorists have indeed issued manifestoes of amazing intellectual power and fervour, veritable lyrics and pæans, so did Proudhon, so did Bakunin, so did Stimer, so did Nietzsche, so, in his own way, did Marx. But the ancient ways of human nature, and the deep laws of human association, rejected these destroying visions, and they will reject that of Syndicalism.

In innumerable passages the new literature echoes, as we have said, the long hatred of Anarchist for Socialist, a hatred which naturally extends itself to politics in general. But the tone has changed. The Syndicalist does not protest so much against what Whitman calls "the insolence of elected persons," as against their economic incompetence. M. Sorel represents the contempt of the craftsman for the mere bureaucrat. Syndicalism stands, even etymologically, for the men trained to some special process, the man who can do some particular thing, and who is full of pride in his skill and his work. M. Sorel, it appears, has condemned *sabotage* in express and passionate terms; to him it is a sort of unpardonable treachery committed by a man against what is best in his own self, as if Rodin were, in a temper, to take a hammer and smash his Balzac. With this pride of the craftsman in his soul Sorel looks with forecasting eye at the spectacle of a committee of Parliamentary orators set to run a steel works, or an engine-shop, or a woollen factory. He shudders, and the comparative popularity of his shudder is of good omen for the future of labour. In general we may say that, while the Syndicalist Utopia is no more possible or desirable than its forerunners, the Syndicalist critique has many valuable elements. At least it helps to lead back the mind of labour from "flapdoodle" revolution to realism, service, and a kind of tonic pride.

The new strategy of Syndicalism is, of course, the general strike. Is it so new? As a speculation it lies in a hundred places all along the literature of social discontent. Sir Arthur Clay has very aptly recalled a crystalizing phrase of Mirabeau's: "Le peuple, dont les seule immobilité serait formidable." Such immobility is imagined in a very concrete form in a very well-known sonnet of Sully Prudhomme which seems, curiously enough, to have been overlooked:

> Le laboureur m'a dit en songe : "Fais ton pain,
> Je ne te nourris plus, gratte la terre et sème,"
> Le tisserand m'a dit : "Fais tes habits toi-même,"
> Et le maçon m'a dit : "Prends la truelle en main,"
> Et seul, abandonné de tout le genre humain,
> Dont je traînais partout l'implacable anathème
> Quand j'implorais du ciel une pitié suprême,
> Je trouvais des yeux, doutant si l'anbe était réelle,
> De hardis compagnons sifflaient sur leur échelle,
> Les métiers bourdonnaient, less champs étaient semés :
> Je connus mon bonheur, et qu'au monde où nous sommes
> Nul ne peut se vauter de se passer des hommes,
> Et depuis ce jour-là je les ai tous aimés.

Sully Prudhomme had his dream, and turned it to excellent purpose ; in our time the experience has come to some of the more timid in the blacker habiliments of a nightmare and has had no better result than to set them babbling of volleys at the pit mouths, and cavalry charges in the factory towns.

The strike is a lamentably old and familiar weapon, and the passage in thought from a single strike to the conception of a general strike is not very difficult. When we come to a passage in reality, however, which is the sole point of interest, the case is very different. It is hard to believe that there can be anywhere a scaremonger so scared as to believe that the dream of Sully Prudhomme has any relation to the actualities of 1912. Such queer people, however, do apparently exist ; if any of them asks why his nightmare is to be so dogmatically dismissed, and why it is impossible, we can only answer that men are not built that way. That a trade union not on strike should sympathise with a trade union on strike is very natural, and in such cases the sympathy in question often takes the shape of a subsidy. But the "sympathetic strike," the mildest prologue imaginable to a general strike, has failed hopelessly in the few instances in which it was tried, as, for example, by the Irish railway men. By the terms of the hypothesis the larger conflict must be inaugurated and directed by the trade unions, and these bodies would not inaugurate if they could, nor could they if they would. And for very good reasons. The unions, powerful though they are, represent but a small fraction of the whole mass of labour. They are, as testified by the late Congress, extremely conservative and pacific: their benefit sections, in contrast to the more revolutionary French organizations, are of enormous importance, and the Insurance Act gives them a greatly increased interest in having the peace kept. But there is a deeper, a more nakedly human bulwark of security. The worker, like everybody else in the community, is, in the first place, a consumer, and a general strike means general starvation. Except in the event of total loss of reason men will not saw through the branch on which not only themselves but their wives and families are supported. So much for Syndicalism in its main features. It might almost be defined as trade unionism in a temper, and in a violent hurry. As for its alleged revolt against politics and the whole working machinery of the State, aud its exclusive reliance on direct action, this is not to be taken very seriously. No man with a heavy weight to lift, and two arms to lift it with, will ever be persuaded to fit himself for his task by deliberately amputating one of them. Nothing is commoner than to find a Syndicalist who, in his first sentence, has abjured the State, proceeding, in his second, to demand a whole code of new laws. Just as many a German votes Socialist solely in order to goad or jog on the more conservative elements on the path of social policy, so a few young and impatient spirits have seized on Syndicalism as a cudgel with which to accelerate the pace of the

LABOUR: WAR OR PEACE?

Parliamentary Labour Party. Time will probably take its revenge on more than one of them by sending them, in due course, into Parliament.

But let us guard against lapsing back into comfortable apathy. It is mere rhetoric to say that our present industrial system has been tried and condemned, but its flaws and distortions have certainly been dramatically unveiled. Impressed by the appalling waste of industrial war business men are everywhere demanding some absolute specific, and guarantee of peace. The demand is Utopian, for no such Economists' Stone is to be found. Compulsory arbitration is plainly impracticable, and if we inquire into the justice of such a scheme we cannot but be surprised to discover that its chief advocates are those who, as against the trade unions, warmly defend the right of the individual labourer to sell or to refuse to sell his work at a given wage. Compulsory arbitration is illusory, for the simple reason that there is not in the nation force sufficient to drive organized labour into mine or factory against its will. Organized labour refuses vehemently, and from its own point of view very properly, to surrender its right to appeal in last resort to the strike, but even without this formal refusal any attempt at coercion must of its nature be futile. The idea of submitting the whole industrial population to military discipline and martial law, and of hanging strikers as you would deserters, is preposterous. But we can hope, and must press strongly for compulsory inquiry into the facts and merits of the dispute. The whole lesson of the history of the great strikes is that it is public opinion which in the end decides the result, and public opinion is entitled in these complex times to the aid of some skilled official tribunal, as distinguished from that of necessarily partisan newspapers, in its attempt to discover the real truth of a trade dispute. But the main hope in this regard lies in a continuance of the conservative attitude of the trade union leaders. They have signified again and again their reluctance to bring the weapon of the strike into play except in extremities. It involves the commission on a large scale of the one unpardonable, economic sin, that of waste. It is a method of barbarism, and, rightly understood, it is not a triumph but a defeat of trade unionism. It is highly creditable to these "paid agitators," as they are sometimes foolishly called, that they should stand so firmly for unpopular sanities as against the blood and thunder insurgents of their own army. In France some of them apparently rise to an even higher plane and question whether "so grave a lesion to the fraternal solidarity of labour" as is involved in the idea of a strike is in strict theory at all justifiable. What comes to be universally perceived is that the commisariat on which labour enters these wars is very meagre, and that the sorest wounds inflicted by a striker are on the striker himself, and his class. All this is to say in other words that the prospect of industrial peace is bound up not with the suppression, but with the extension of trade unions. We may echo dogmatically the maxim of Professor Pigou that the employer who fights against recognition is always wrong. Nor is there either wisdom or any germ of success in the attempt to strangle the realities of trade unionism with laws or legal decisions. It is easy to elaborate a fine-drawn argument showing that the unions occupy a position of privilege, and even tyranny. There is even a glimmer of truth in the complaint. Unanimity of action is of the very essence of their policy, and a union has to choose between absolute supremacy in its own particular trade or ineffectiveness. The rationale of what might otherwise be questioned stands clearly expressed in history and experience. It cannot be better put than in the

authoritative words of Professor R. T. Ely, the
distinguished American economist:

> "Whatever bad traits naturally characterize
> labour organizations are aggravated so long as they
> are obliged to struggle for existence. Whenever
> the fact of their right to exist is frankly acknow-
> ledged, and employers, ceasing to persecute them
> or their officials, recognize the man who treats in
> a representative capacity for the sale of the
> commodity labour as courteously as they would
> an agent for the sale of corn or wheat; finally,
> whenever courts cease to harrow them with legal
> chicanery, as courts long did in England, they tend
> to become strong and conservative."

When we come to consider suggested modifications
of the wage-system our task becomes very formidable.
It can be attempted in these pages only in a very
bald and summary fashion. All the proposed schemes
aim at altering the arrangement which at present
embattles labour and capital in two mutually hostile
camps. In all of them the shaping idea is to give
the industrial worker an interest in the prosperity
of the capital employed in his industry, and they
arrange themselves in a regular hierarchy in pro-
portion to the size of that interest. In the first
type we have the wage-system in its pure form; in
the second, profit-sharing, we have that system
modified by giving the worker a share in the profits,
but not in the capital or the control of the enterprise; in the third, co-partnership, the worker acquires
in addition to his wages a share, allocated by way
of annual bonus, either in the capital alone or, in
the more advanced stage, in both capital and control;
and the final term of the process is reached in co-
operative production, in which capital and labour
coalesce in the same body of workers. The under-

lying principle of all these reconstructions is obviously endowed with a peculiar fascination. To get rid of an enemy, or rather of his enmity, by enlisting him for service under your own colours is an attractive prospect. Generous minds have constantly revolted against the notion of one man selling himself or hiring himself, body and sonl, as they phrase it, to another. Certain Catholic writers, especially in Austria, have attempted by a subtle but unconvincing analysis to represent the relation between employer and employed, not as contractual, but as associational. But are these schemes workable, and, if they are, do they afford an adequate specific for social unrest? Professor Chapman has, with his customary wisdom, been lately asking us to approach such solutions, and indeed all solutions of a great difficulty, in an absolutely non-doctrinaire spirit. We must look at them in a realistic and concrete way, studying particular facts rather than hastily formulating universal laws.

With regard to all these modes of association we have considerable experience to guide us. Profit-sharing assumes either of two forms; in the one the employer formally contracts to divide, annually or bi-annually, a percentage of the profits of the business among the employees; in the other there is no formal engagement, but, as a matter of practice, wages are supplemented by the voluntary grant of bonuses. This latter method of increasing at once the efficiency and the peacefulness of labour is very general, especially in the world of commerce, but its scope is obviously very limited. It does not create any genuine association; it comprises the integrity of that collective bargaining which is the essence of trade unionism; and it has a tendency to sap the independence of the worker. In fact, Professor Gide, commenting on the schedule of bonuses allowed in the factory of Van Marken at Delft—a

notable case in point—observes that it reduces grown
men to the level of " schoolboys to whom marks are
allotted for good conduct." Sometimes this system
is superimposed on the formal engagement. Of the
latter, and of the whole device in general, Mr. D. F.
Selloss, our greatest authority, takes a view far from
flattering. Profit-sharing, he observes, has been in
operation in these countries for more than half a
century, but it has rarely succeeded, and in a great
many cases has had to be abandoned. Its weak-
nesses are patent. From the point of view of capital
it must always seem absurd that labour should share
in the profit but not in the losses of an enterprise.
The workers on their part complain that the profits
divided among them have first to be earned by extra
intensity of labour—they are a sort not of overtime
but of over-toil payment; if an enterprise can afford
an increased dividend to labour it had better come
in the form of a rise in wages; and, finally, even in
favourable circumstances the income accruing under
the head of profits is so trivial in comparison with
that accruing under the head of wages that no real
synthesis of the interests of labour with those of
capital is effected. On this last rock we have
seen many schemes go to pieces in recent years.
An examination of any striking success confirms its
importance. In the case of the Suez Canal Company,
for instance, we are told that the employees are so
devoted that when the telegraph board announces
an increase in the number of vessels that have passed
through during the day the whole staff claps hands.
Enquiry shows that the profits shared by this
company amount to no less than 30 to 40 per cent.
of the wages. Co-partnership, now becomes the
fetish of some writers, promises better, but unhappily,
experience does not uniformly confirm its promises.
Did it possess the almost miraculous virtues ascribed
to it, it must by this time have covered with its

sheltering branches a great part of the industrial world ; for the *Familistère* of Godin at Guise dates back almost to the inauguration of British Free Trade. Successes are to be chronicled in that instance, in the woollen factory of Mr. Cooke Taylor at Batley, in the Cash Register establishment at Dayton, Ohio, in the printing firm of Van Marken at Delft, and in the London gas companies. In this last instance it is significant to note that the managements found it necessary to compel the workers to acquire a share in the capital. But, despite the brilliant and widely celebrated success of these experiments, the co-partnership idea has not greatly expanded; it seems neither to gain ground nor to lose it. Co-operative production is in no better case. As a plan of organization for the whole of industry it amounts substantially to the impossible dream of the Syndicalists-Socialists. As a type among the other types of enterprise it lies under two main disadvantages, the difficulty of obtaining capital and that of maintaining discipline. In agriculture it undoubtedly possesses the secret of the future, but there it becomes a phenomenon of a different order. In manufacturing industry it is apparently able to hold its ground only when it rests on a basis of associations of consumers, confines the co-operative formula to the side of capital, and employs labour under the discipline of the present wage-system. Its one notable triumph of late, the Glass-Workers' Association of Albi, turned largely on subsidies and preferences granted, mainly on political grounds, by public bodies and "Co-operatives of Consumption." Other experiments have been tried, particularly what Mr. Lever of Port Sunlight calls "prosperity-sharing." This is the programme of the palace factory and the garden city. In every instance in which employers have followed Mr. Lever's plan of humanizing the conditions of labour, surrounding their workers with comfort and even a hint of luxury, they have been amply repaid. Advocates have also appeared in the field on behalf of an intermediate plan by which not the individual worker but the trade union would acquire considerable blocks of the capital of their industries. Others propound a scheme under which the workers, or groups of them, would take jobs on piece-rates from the employer, and apportion among themselves both the labour and the remuneration.

There is none of these proposals that is not worthy of consideration. Any one of them may, in some particular trade in some particular place, be the best path to peace and development. But any such association seems to demand exceptional personality, and an exceptional tradition. Everything indicates that it is likely to appear only as a happy accident, and that the normal type of enterprise will continue to be based on the wage-system. What we have got to realize, to absorb into our social philosophy, to get into our bones, as the phrase is, is that the wage-system as at present in operation is profoundly unsatisfactory. It must be amended if it is to endure. The standard of wages is, in general, too low; over a great area it is so low as to shut out the recipients of it, not only from the amenities but even from the necessaries of life. This undenied fact is the lion in the path. The worker is under a further disadvantage, which has manifested itself very prominently in his recent history; he makes his contract of service, not in terms of the economic realities which he needs —food, clothes and shelter—but in terms of an economic symbol, money. If the fluctuations of the latter are unfavourable to him he finds the whole sense of his agreement gone, while the latter remains. If he disregards that he is in danger of estranging public opinion by what is represented as a breach of faith. There is yet another characteristic of the

171

personal wage-history of the wage-earner. Unlike the public functionary, or the mental labourer in general, he does not enjoy an income which rises steadily if slowly, offering automatic provision for the responsibilities of marriage, and the growing disabilities of age. The wage-earner reaches his maximum early, stays there during maturity, to slip lamentably down as his hair blanches. Nothing could well be more pathetic than the recorded fact that in some English industrial towns the unusual consumption of hair-dye has been traced not to feminine coquetry, but to the desperate attempts of ageing workers to conceal their age. Nor must it be forgotten that the majority of them have had to support their manhood on a wage which made thrift not only impossible but almost criminal. To what measures are we to look for amelioration? The first essential is a change of mind; there must be a deliberate adhesion, not a mere grudging and forced assent, to the principle that the level of real wages in all but all industries, but especially in those in which labour is not organized, is too low for social health or stability, and that it must rise. The divergence of nominal from real wages is mainly a matter of terminology. We have simply got to recognize that every collective agreement fixing the price of labour is controlled by a *rebus sic stentibus* proviso. A rise in real wages is the substantial end to be attained, and the attainment of it is the solution of the social problem. The mode of attainment most widely discussed at present is the establishment, by law, of a minimum wage in every industry. This proposal has encountered many criticisms, the most surprising being to the effect that it is revolutionary and Socialistic. The truth is that it proposes merely to extend to unorganized labour, through the machinery of the State, what organized labour has obtained through trade unionism. And so far is this scheme

from being Socialistic, that on the Continent it is
specially identified with the Catholic School of
Economics, although it must be said that so
distinguished a theorist as Rombaud prefers a
customary to a statutory wage. Will industry
everywhere be able to bear forthwith a minimum
high enough to constitute a genuine living wage?
Mr. Ramsay MacDonald has a short way of dealing
with this fundamental difficulty. If any industry is
not able to do so, let it perish; it is a mere parasite,
a national loss rather than an asset. Such a dictum
is hopelessly at war with realities, and with the
realistic temper of mind, which alone can achieve
lasting results. There are literally thousands of
instances in which the customary wage is, for the
time being, less than a genuine living wage; in which,
for the time being, no better is possible; and yet the
destruction of which would be nothing less than
insanity. The universal establishment of a human
minimum is, indeed, the ideal towards which we
must work. But we must come to it by a steady
process of amelioration, not by a sudden stroke of
Utopianism. Any Minimun Wage Act must be
indefinitely flexible: permitted variations from place
to place, and perhaps a sliding-scale arrangement
must enable it to adjust itself to the varying
actualities to which it is applied. So framed, it
offers itself, if not as a panacea, at least as a
promising experiment. As for the other peculiar
difficulties of the wage-earner's life (arising from
sickness, unemployment and age), the State has
already intervened. And we may take it for granted
that, whatever details may be corrected in the light
of experience, the area of social legislation is bound
not to contract, but to widen.

Such more or less mechanical readjustments must
come, but unless there is in the community a sufficient reserve of good-will to keep the wheels oiled,

we cannot expect them to function very smoothly.
It is no mere rhetoric that appeals for a change of
spirit. We have already chronicled it as a good
omen that the worker is beginning to recover his
pride of craftsmanship, and to discover that to bear
burdens, although toilsome, is a toil of honour. He
may well desire that a similar pride in tasks accomplished and duties loyally fulfilled should find
expression among the wealthier classes. A world
in which everybody proclaims his grievances and
forgets his obligations must necessarily rock with
unrest. We have all got to accept life as a hard
but cleansing discipline, of which effort, after painful
effort, is the normal texture, and pleasure but a rare
embroidery. In the restoration of such a sane social
philosophy it is often announced that the Church
has a great part to play. To me it seems that the
sanctuary and the laboratory of the Church is the
individual conscience. There are good grounds for
adding to the curriculum of ecclesiastical colleges a
course in economics, and the social sciences in
general. A priest with spare time can help greatly
towards peace, not by lecturing his people—as a
rule with more fervour than insight—but by reason-
ing out with them in quiet conference the significance
of the economic conditions among which their lot is
cast. On that line much, and very much, can be
done. But any attempt to formulate in the name
of the Church a rigorous and exclusive social programme, and to insist that that is sound Catholic
policy, must, of its nature, be futile and even dangerous.
It is indeed part of the mission of the Church to
safeguard those ethical truths which lie at the basis
of all society ; but when it comes to a discussion of
the technical processes of society, economic and political, every man must effect his own synthesis of principle and technique, and he must be free to follow the
light of his own conscience and his own experience.

THE WORLD OF THE BLIND

War has long been accepted as our best aid to the teaching of geography: blood is an expensive marking fluid for maps, but it is vivid and indelible. Through its virtue alone have the Egypts, the Tibets, and the Koreas been opened to general vision. And it would seem as if a similar passage through calamity to knowledge will fall to be recorded in regard to that most secret province of all, the World of the Blind. Mr. Pearson, a great master of journals, is stricken with this ancient affliction. Immediately his vast power is thrown behind the organization which has so long been labouring towards a true understanding of it. The public attention is fixed. We resolve to be no longer blind to blindness, but set about what is at once a study and a campaign. Mr. Pearson has transformed his personal misfortune into a source of light and promise.

In such circumstances any elucidation of the psychological process that goes on behind closed eyes is valuable, but a report proceeding from the centre of that obscure world possesses a very special value. If the author of that account from within be, as well, a trained observer, a writer already distinguished, and a man of genuine scientific balance, his book ceases to be a document that may or may not be read. It imposes itself. All these conditions are amply fulfilled in *Le Monde des Aveugles*[1] of M. Pierre Villey. Self-analysis by the blind is no new phenomenon; no one is likely to forget, for instance, the almost ecstatic quality of the writings of Helen Keller, or the provocative interest of her revelations.

[1] *Flammarion, Paris*, 1914.

But with M. Villey we enter another order of literature. Trained on Braille, and using it as his material
apparatus of communication, he has on the one hand
become master of a deep general culture, and on the
other he has produced a calm, exact, reasoned, and
in all points convincing examination of the mental
processes of his fellow-blind. His book is a veritable
Baedeker of the veiled country in which they dwell.
It is a notable step from myth and legend to reality.

For, indeed, there is no strangeness of human
experience about which the mythopoeic faculty has
more eagerly woven its webs. This exile from the
sun is so dramatic, so absolute in its blackness, as to
incite any imagination. That incitement is doubled
when it is discovered that a calamity which seems
the end of everything does not end everything, but
that the blind manage to move about, to live, and
even to be useful in a world of the seeing. In
primitive civilizations this miracle is ascribed to
special commerce with the gods. The man from
whom the visible has been withdrawn is recognized
as the seer of the invisible and the diviner of the
future. Such are in the Greek story Tiresias and
even Homer himself. In Korea to-day the blind are
respected as exorcists, magicians, and healers. In
Turkey they are valued as reciters of the Koran on
ceremonial occasions, and their prayers are beyond
all others acceptable to Allah. In Russia the proverb
runs that "God Himself is the teacher of the blind,
and His works are made manifest in them." In
modern communities the legend assumes a different
form. Artistically it is employed as a unique symbol
by the pessimists. Synge, for example, finds it a fit
vessel in which to dip out that Marah-water which
he finds in his "Well of the Saints." In popular
science, or rather the unexamined hearsay that passes
for science, it appears as an exaggeration of those
faculties which are not impaired by the loss of sight.

THE WORLD OF THE BLIND

The blind distinguish colours by touch independently of texture. They play cards with great success, especially when they themselves are the dealers, for they feel accurately the whole hands of their opponents. They carve statues, are king's tailors, and duke's coachmen. They know by the trot of a horse that he is blind, and distinguish one pigeon from another by the mere sound of its wings. In music especially they are supreme. Every blind person is a potential, if not an actual, fiddler; a marvellous talent is at all events native in them and universal. M. Villey, who refers us for these traditionary anecdotes to writers so little tainted with "credulity," as Bayle, Diderot, and Garnier, and to a *Biography of the Blind* by James Wilson, does not attempt to sift them in detail; he sets the whole mass aside as belonging to the sphere of *légendes abracadabrantes*. He proceeds upon the sounder basis of laboratory exploration and scientifically examined records of actual experience. Brushing aside all legends, he is concerned to establish two positions, first, that the blind person is not necessarily in respect of any sense or faculty a genius of any kind, and second, that he is just as little of necessity an idiot of any kind. To M. Villey the most difficult task before his blind is that of merely living, of earning the bread of independence: the more their mentality is misunderstood, whether by way of exaggeration or the reverse, the more difficult does that task become. Almost with passion he repudiates as *a priori* absurd the notion that four senses are better than five. Any special refinement, say of touch or hearing, that may manifest itself is due solely to a narrower localization of attention. Sight being the sense of distractions, and essentially vagrant and diffuse, the closing-up of it may predispose to a more concentrated inner life, but in general the only principle involved is that of intensive culture of a faculty. And, however exceptionally endowed a blind snbject may be, he must always be a sense short. With equal passion, however, M. Villey begs us not to argue from this to a mutilated personality. In the ordinary case the normal mind, and the whole mind, is there behind the diminished apparatus of perception. The world of space can be adequately realized through tactile impressions. If necessarily somewhat limited as regards freedom of movement, the healthy blind can nevertheless be delivered, by appropriate education, from complete helplessness even in that regard. They can be trained up to be economically inde-penndent, and not mere pitiable parasites. No intellectual or moral idea is inaccessible to them. Given the material apparatus of instruction, in the shape mainly of a sufficient equipment of Braille finger-language books, they can build a line of com-munication to any section of general culture. It is to be understood that this claim is made only where blindness is the sole disability. Where graver lesions of the organism, and especially of the brain, are involved, we are commonly in presence of a pheno-menon of mental as well as of physical defectiveness, and due allowance must be made.

The psychology of the blind raises three central points of controversy: the acuteness of the senses taken singly, the substitution of the missing sense of vision by one or more of the others, and the adequacy of the four-sense apparatus to the interpre-tation of reality as given. The first is a measurable problem of psycho-physics. The evidence of the laboratory is alone conclusive, or it would be but for a weakness on which M. Villey lays a shrewd finger. "Our instruments think : they share our prejudices." The æsthesiometer, to cite the simplest, yields different results according to the sharpness of its points and the substance of which the compass legs

are made. A more serious element of error is introduced by the character of the subjects available for
examination. There is blindness and blindness. In
some instances the vision, and only the vision, is
affected. In others the brain, the spinal cord, and
the whole nervous system are disturbed and debili-
tated by some grave organic lesion. To classify all
these together under the common rubric of "the
blind " is plainly to invite wide-ranging discrepancies.
Since that is precisely what has been done, it is not
surprising to find two opinions in the field. On the
one side, Griesbach and Kunz claim to have shown
by a series of many thousand experiments that the
sensibility of the blind is in no respect superior and
is in very many respects inferior to that of the
seeing. They established no difference as regards
hearing or smell. To tactile impressions they judge
the blind to be less acutely responsive. Strangely
enough, they found the hand, and, of the hand, the
index or reading finger, to be eminently the area of
inferiority. On the other side the superiority of the
blind, having long been accepted as an axiom, has
not failed to secure laboratory confirmation by
Czemak, Goltz, Gastner, Hocheisen, and Stern.
Laura Bridgman, possessing only the single sense
of touch, would seem bound *a priori* to excel in tactile
sensibility: actual measurement showed it to be two
or three times the normal. But strangely enough,
Helen Keller, examined in a more coldly scientific
spirit, exhibited no notable superiority. M. Villey,
grasping the controversy, as it were, from within as
well as from without, is convinced that, other organic
conditions being equal, no relation of superiority
and inferiority can be scientifically established.
Blindness does not induce either a general stupor
or a general exhaltation of the other senses.

The *nisi intellectus ipse* by the addition of which
Leibnitz corrected Locke's *Nihil est in intellectu quod*

non ante fuerit in sensu is to M. Villey the key to the whole business. Not in the perceiving sense but in the interpreting mind does the true centre of difference reside. The only "miracle" with which we are confronted is that of specialized attention and memory. These are the most familiar activities of conscious life, and are the matter of a hundred text-book instances. An officer will detect at the first glance at a line of soldiers an irregularity of uniform or equipment which would escape an hour's conscientious scrutiny by a layman. To a European newly landed in the East all Chinamen seem the same; in two or three days he has already begun to distinguish individuals. In each case it is not the eye but the mind that sees more. The datum of sense is received into a richer associational mass and more swiftly construed. The stream of consciousness, impinging on a narrower area, strikes that area with more urgent force. Blindness, then, as a condition of mental life, is for all the world like the closing of a lock-gate. There is no intensification of the individual senses, but there is an enhanced rapidity of interpretation. The vicariate of the senses, as M. Villey styles it, presents itself to him under an image which is very clear and suggestive:

"We must not see in it, as is too often supposed, a sort of estate which, on the death of one brother, is divided among his four surviving brothers. Rather do I see it as a workshop, suddenly deserted by one of its artizans, the most active and intelligent of all, one of those aristocrats of labour who by sheer weight of superior ability reduce the initiative of their fellows almost to zero and lay hold of the effective direction of affairs. Confronted with the enormous increase of their burdens the survivors may doubtless give way to despair, and reduce concurrently their own efforts and rewards and the total volume of production. But, on the other hand, if they are men of courage, they may redouble their efforts, and, profiting by the imperious need of their employer, greatly improve their material situation. Were their comrade, instead of leaving, simply to turn over to them part of his task, an identical result might be reached " (p. 70).

The exploitation of the senses proceeds under a sort of Ricardian law of rent. The most profitable, that of vision, naturally comes first into use, and always yields the maximum return. But, under the pressure of circumstances, the margin of cultivation widens, and even the poorest outlying province of perception is made to support life. The normal man, lord of five senses, is free to squander a great part of his less valuable resources. Strip his heritage to four as with M. Villey, to two as with Helen Keller, to one as with Laura Bridgman, and you find the reply of life and genius in what may be called, if you choose, a deepening " miracle " of concentration. Where a blind person does possess a congenital acuteness in any mode of perception, that mode is, of course, likely to play a rôle of proportional importance. *Le Monde des Aveugles* abounds in verified modern examples. For Marie Heurtin, as for Helen Keller, every person of her acquaintance has a special odour as recognizable as the perfume of a flower. She never makes a mistake. Sent to the sewing-room with a message to one of her companions, she stands there on her arrival slowly turning her head and sniffing the air, until she locates her goal. M. Yves Guégan, who is completely deaf, knows that the post has come by the smell of the postman's letter-bag which he detects on the floor next below him. In a series of experiments he was able to determine his precise position in a room, but lost this power as soon as his nostrils were closed with small rubber-faced pincers. A severe cold in the head had the same disabling influence as the pincers. This subtle mastery of odour, combined with the guidance afforded by muscular memory, enables him to find his way almost freely about the town of Brest where he resides. In the sphere of touch M. Villey's explanation dissolves into simplicity the "marvels" which so strongly impress certain seeing observers. Fluent reading from Braille, involving as it does the perception through the index finger of more than two thousand raised dots per minute, is on analysis no more amazing than, say, piano-playing by the normal person. The printing of the matter read involves the two thousand dots, but they have not been cognized in detail. A small, scattered minority of them is sufficient to "spring the imagination," as Meredith's phrase has it, to stir the associational mass in the mind behind the finger. Perhaps the most striking example of a very unpromising area of perception fructified by deliberate attention is afforded by the blind deaf mutes. Sight and sound as such are forbidden to them, but they learn to detect the minutest vibratory movements involved in these phenomena. The least change in temperature or the lightest undulation of a column of air is laid hold of by them and developed into a far from ineffective guide. M. Guégan, for instance, recognizes his friends by the vibrations "produced by the impact of their feet on the ground."

"I never cross a street," he writes, "without stopping for some seconds to assure myself that no vehicle is passing: this I judge from the vibrations of the ground under my feet. These are to me a fruitful source of information; I perceive them so clearly that I have the illusion of actually hearing."

The mythology of the subject has uniformly ascribed to the blind a sixth sense, sometimes represented as the sense of orientation, sometimes

as that of obstacles. Certain psychologists, like
M. Woelfflin, have not only believed that there is
such a sense, but they have even located it for its
physiological base in the *nervus trigeminus*. But
upon the non-existence of any such compensation
M. Villey is sharply definite. It is true, we learn
from him, that many blind persons claim to be
conscious of a sort of *toucher à distance*, a new order
of sensation experienced mainly about the temples.
But on examination the evidence is found to be
inconclusive. In many instances, whether the subject be blind or seeing, some cutaneous affection such
as scarlatina or smallpox will be found to have
produced hyper-aesthesia. In the remainder the
sixth sense is no more than a more sensitive interpretation of the data normally given, especially of
those of temperature, odour, and undulation.

Among the most fascinating of his chapters is that
in which M. Villey discusses the possibility of
attaining, through purely tactile impressions, an
adequate perception of space. Such a question
clearly plunges us *en pleine métaphysique*, and runs
down to the foundations of epistemology. According
to an authority like Platner, the blind perceive
extension under the form, not of space, but of time.
Between them and the seeing there is fixed a gulf
which can never be crossed. To the fantastic
geometries of four dimensions must be added
another still stranger, the geometry of the blind.
Such a view receives no support from the author
of *Le Monde des Aveugles*. The problem of the
Many and the One, the passage from concrete and
multiple impressions to the generic idea, is no doubt
worked out more painfully in terms of touch than in
those of sight. But the process of elaboration leaves
the sightless also in possession of images "extended,
synthetic, extremely supple and mobile." It is a
sort of tactile vision.

"The word *sight* alone seems adequate to those apparitions which surge through the mind, free from any admixture of purely muscular sensations, from any representation through the fingers or the hands, less rich, less complex, considerably less extended than visual ideas, but like them at the same time one and many, grasped in their integrity and in their details by the inner eye of consciousness " (p. 167).

The difference of modality does not prevent the conquest of the same substantial result. The procedure of touch is analytical and successive, whereas that of vision is synthetic and instantaneous. But when the material given in perception has been, so to say, chewed over by the mind, it undergoes a transformation. Memory brings back an object not fragmentarily, but in a flash:

"It is not a *défilé*, a successive unfolding, however rapid, of representations in which the different parts are added one to the other in the order in which they were first experienced. It is a fountaining forth (*jaillissement*). The object recurs *en bloc*."

If we turn to the degree of mastery of practical life which modern educational apparatus permits a blind person to attain, at least in favourable circumstances, we come on many interesting facts. One of M. Villey's correspondents is a commercial traveller who makes long railway journeys without any disagreeable incident. Many others are musicians, especially organists. M. Béraud, of Marseilles, works with success as an electrician; M. Démonet, of Vichy, is a prosperous piano-maker. It would, however, be a mere illusion of optimism to suppose that in any of these skilled pursuits the real handicap of blindness has been wholly overcome. M. Villey himself has made a distinguished mark in literature, and, what is even more remarkable, in the literature of erudition. He is one of the best-known Montaigne scholars. His edition of the *Essais* is, in the full sense of the word, monumental. He has followed, with the most minute care, the track of Montaigne's reading and has reconstructed, almost year by year, a history of his mind and imagination. It goes without saying that in this huge task he had the aid of secretaries and friends, but, when all that has been taken into account, it remains an astonishing achievement. Accomplished critic that he is, M. Villey is at his best in his analysis of the art life possible to the blind, both creative and appreciative. He introduces us to a blind German novelist of great merit, Oskar Baum, author of *Das Leben im Dunkeln*, and to a French poetess, Mme. Galeron. He examines passages from Flaubert and Hugo, and finds them curiously independent of visual sensations, almost wholly compacted of sound and movement. In the lyrical pages of Helen Keller he is sorry to discover at many points mere verbalism, or even psittacism. Most of all does he distrust her claim to penetrate into the spirit and meaning of sculpture through the medium of touch. For him, visible beauty is a world shut hopelessly against the blind. From the reports of the seeing they may, indeed, construct some vague notion of such a reality, but this is far from constituting any real knowledge of it. The gates of that Eden are closed against them.

But much is open. How much, one hardly understands until one has accompanied this humane and gracious scholar in his survey of a strange world. The long educational effort extending through Haüy and Braille down to our own time has delivered these disinherited from isolation and restored them to human intercourse. The pathos of their affliction is no longer intolerable. If they accept the conditions set them in the noble spirit that breathes through *Le Monde des Aveugles*, they are lifted into a sort of mountain-air of morality : they wear their calamity like a crown.

THE DAY'S BURDEN

I cannot think of any single piece of work that would help to an understanding of the blind so greatly as an English translation of this book. M. Villey's scientific equipment is at all points adequate. He has produced a chapter of comparative psychology of a new order, and of unique value. It is a clear addition to the weight of evidence in support of the spiritual interpretation of conscious life as against the meaner theories of empiricism. Everywhere we come upon a soul straining painfully for expression behind the mutilated organs of sense, but it is an integral soul.

As I have said, the scientific interest of M. Villey's work is touched throughout with a warm glow of emotion. A great wind of loneliness blows through it; you are made aware of the more than feminine passion for sympathy of these *gens incompris* of our kind. But behind all is the desire that the seeing may understand in order that they may help. Not the almoner but the educator, not "institutional treatment," as our chilly phrase has it—with its leading-strings, and crutches, and uniforms, and big refectories smelling of shell-cocoa—but, as far as possible, the life of the economically independent citizen, such is the burden of M. Villey's appeal. How far is it realizable? The results of an enquiry undertaken in 1905 into the progress of 264 pupils of the *Institution Nationale des Jeunes Aveugles*, are suggestive. Of these 64 had been obliged to return home after their school course; 30 of them were able to make some contribution to the household budget, but the remainder were, through disease or inferiority of intelligence, entirely dependent. A second group of 94 just contrived to support a celibate existence. Some of them were obliged from time to time to apply for assistance, but *per contra* some also were found to be almost well-to-do. Forty per cent., that is to say, 106, had married, and were enjoying the normal life of domesticity. Of these 16 had failed in the struggle, 18 were unable to keep going without occasional help from the Institution, but the remaining 72 had made their way, and 30 of them were very comfortable. In all 85 per cent. had discovered in our economic organization some niche into which they fitted. The figures, it should be added, relate exclusively to males.

A curious feature noted is that, subjectively, this success is felt to be greater than in its objective self it actually is. Many of the pupils came from the poorest sections of the labouring classes: their physical affliction procured for them an education far superior to that available for their healthier brothers and sisters, and on leaving school they took their places several stages higher in the hierarchy of industry. Many of them go so far as to refer to their blindness as a "happy accident," a "providential calamity," and so on. The more naïve and self-sufficient, indeed, develop in regard to their relatives all the symptoms of the thorough snob.

The occupations to which the specialized education of the blind leads them to gravitate have already been indicated. We may set aside as freaks of genius the more astonishing of the cases on record. True, we do find at Marseilles M. Béraud working successfully as an electrical engineer. He has, unaided except by an apprentice, planned and erected many installations, private and ecclesiastical. At the Paris Automobile Exhibition of 1910 he took down, repaired, and set up again many motor vehicles. At the automobile trials of Ventouse in 1911 a tandem motor bicycle, built in part by himself, with his mechanic as pilot and himself as passenger, obtained second prize. Similar, though less impressive, is the work of M. Moünnich at Magdeburg. We have details of a blind brewer who

exercised his profession with considerable success
for ten years, of a blind cut-glass worker, of a blind
vine-dresser whose skill had become a tradition of
his country-side. M. Villey himself personally
examined the case of a blind cutler, recently dead,
at Vichy. Under the eyes of our author he performed all the most difficult processes of his trade.
What most impressed M. Villey was the infallible
precision with which he put together the component
pieces, six or seven in number, of his knife-hafts,
already shaped by himself in ivory, horn, copper, or
iron. A M. Person, also at Paris, had arrived, and
believed that any blind mechanic could arrive, at a
complete mastery of clock-cleaning and repairing.
But, in M. Villey's reasoned judgment, success in
such enterprises demands a " conspiracy of benevo-
lence " in addition to a marked originality which is
by no means the general heritage of the blind. He
found further, on investigation of the "documented "
marvels, that in practically no instance was the
blind mechanic, however well he worked, able to
work fast enough to earn his living. In other
branches in which less skill is required, and in which
special training operates as a set-off against the
natural advantage of the seeing, the prospect is much
more hopeful. Chief of these are music, and the
industries associated with it. As is well-known, the
teaching of music has long occupied a prominent
place in the curriculum of the blind, and this study
is so neglected in normal schools that something
approximating to a fair start is possible. The
natural faculty of the blind pupil is so fully evoked
as to transform a *minus* into a *plus*. Very many
blind persons of both sexes have made their way as
organists, music-teachers, and even minor com-
posers. The less fine talents attempted, against
the advice of their educators, piano-tuning, with the
slight grasp of mechanics involved, and from that

passed on to piano-building, and in certain cases to furniture-making. Of this class the success of genius is that of M. Démonet. He acquired a decaying piano-factory, and in one year more than restored its former prosperity. His story, which is too long for minute narration, approaches more nearly than any of the others to the fairy-tale. Its special interest is that it centres in a domain for which the blind are specialized, and in which, in all the capacities enumerated, they have in large numbers succeeded. Medical massage is yet another of these particular areas. The "more scientific fingers" of the blind, that touch which has long been legendary, find in massage an occupation that literally plays into their hand. And as massage becomes a more and more popular treat-ment, and as the employment of a blind masseuse or masseur enables a lady or gentleman of fashion to gratify without any extra expense the two passions of curiosity and pity, it would seem to be a career with a future. The teaching of modern languages is another avenue of promise opened by a change of method. Living languages are now learned not from dead print but from living speech. With appropriate training the memory of a blind pupil of a linguistic turn can easily be stocked with adequate material of instruction. The Braille system opens a way, though a narrow way, into the garden of litera-ture. The demand for the teaching of modern languages grows every year, and all these are favour-able influences. At the same time the attainment of a position in the world of erudition comparable to that of M. Villey's must continue to be a phenom-enon as rare as it is precious.

The whole task before us is the adaptation of the blind to their economic environment. It is not enough to spend benevolently : the State and private philanthropists must also spend intelligently. The blind fiddler, led about by his faithful dog, and the blind osier-weaver and basket-maker, do not exhaust the field of proved possibility. A more valuable help towards ths new programme than *Le Monde des Aveugles* I cannot easily imagine. On the one side it is the science and the politics of blindness; on the other its most poignant because its most penetrating literature. We have been accustomed to speak of the blind leading the blind as a counter-sense. In M. Villey there enters a blind man who also leads the seeing.

A MAN TROUBLED ABOUT EVERYTHING

My drowse had already been shattered by a sharp click on the pavement of the verandah. Then, as a chair was pushed back with that crunching creak, which is the least tolerable of all domestic noises, I turned to my neighbour.

"You have lost your pipe?"

Together we found it. He borrowed my tobacco pouch—the ritual of initiation into friendship. He stared with dead eyes into the fires and darknesses of a sea, caressed by a headland, wooded down to the shore, and said heavily:

"It is good to find a lost pipe, but it is easy. I have lost something else that I do not think even the Paduan Saint Anthony will find for me: *I have lost my Table of Values.*"

"Are you a worshipper at the shrine of the idyllic cabbage?" I asked, "and are they food values? Or a painter, and are they colour values? Or a mere stockbroker, left without a key to the madness of the money page in this evening's paper?"

"I speak," he went on, "of what I would call life values, if that vocable 'life' had any clear meaning. Those two-column arrangements of experience into Good and Bad, Good and Better . . . . a more important distinction . . . . Right and Wrong, Aye and No."

"Have you applied to your Party Whips?" I pursued. "A friend of mine always gets his there ready made. Very reasonably, too. Of course they don't always fit at the shoulders as well as the tailored article. But they keep out the cold, and keep you out of it? Have you tried the Bishop of London? Or Mr. Garvin? Or the Militants? Or Mr. Ramsay Macdonald? Or Mr. Bernard Shaw, to mention whom—I omit Messieurs Belloc and Chesterton—is now a recognized duty in conversation? Or, greatest of English names, Mr. F. E. Smith? There are no flies of doubt to spoil the soup of certainty for any of these people. They know."

My companion almost slipped into anger, but caught himself short on the brink.

"Of the Militants," he said, "let us not speak either in praise or blame. Who am I that I should refuse the epic duel of sex? I am not greedy: I do not ask for woman's wisdom, only for man's. That gaitered contradiction, the Bishop of London, is of no use to me, nor that candent Scotchman, who thinks himself a Socialist while he is only a metaphysician. Shaw bores me: besides, he is a hippo-cerf. Mr. Smith's manners are so bad that even if he had the secret of eternal life I should decline to be saved under the barking monosyllable of his opprobrious name. Mr. Garvin is a squirrel. Here he is now, cracking nuts among the fallen leaves. Your eyes quit him for a moment, and when you see him again he is perched on some quite ridiculous tree, looking as debonair and dogmatic about his new posture as he was about his old. Party Whips are good as far as they go. I do not want to see them slain at the crossing of the ways, and the world swaggering into anarchism. But there is no ultimacy in them. Their function is—if you follow me— soaked in relativity?"

When a large metaphysical boulder of this kind is hurled at you it is discreet to be offensive, and, if possible, literary.

"Balzac," I observed, "recounts in one of his

novels what he calls *the pursuit of the absolute.* Pursuit and pursuer end, I seem to remember, in a commodious lunatic asylum, agreeably situated in a well-kept forest."

"Yes! they attain certainty in these places," he mused, "but the price is too big. A lunatic, observe, is a person who is quite sure about one thing, and that thing is wrong. I had a friend who was quite sure that he was a poached egg. They had to upholster his chair with dry toast in order to induce him to sit down. To attain that certainty about a right thing, and without the expense and bother of going mad, is just my problem."

"Is it not possible," I asked, still smarting, "to live on the accumulations of history, and the momentum of civilization? Just keep up with the band, you know?"

"There are so many bands and so many airs! I can't march to infinity in all directions at the same time. Besides it is undignified to drown the music of the soul in somebody else's tin whistle!"

"What are you chiefly troubled about?"

"I am chiefly troubled about everything," came his reply, somewhat brusquely. "The world sets me the conundrum : Christianity or . . . . or . . . . or the other thing? I am, as they say, at heart a Christian. But I read a twelve-and-sixpenny book blowing it sky-high . . . . a good metaphor that, by the way. How can anything be true enough to withstand the assault of a twelve-and-sixpenny book? Then I read another twelve-and-sixpenny book in defence of it, usually by a German professor. I end by not knowing even what Christianity is. Then the world says : Marriage or . . . . or the other thing. I am all for indissoluble marriage. But people send me pamphlets. Here in this very hotel I meet a lady, a most charming lady, who assures me that unless divorce is made cheap, private, and almost automatic she will be forced to poison her husband, a most estimable man with a splendid golf temperament."

"Hard lines on her," I managed to interpolate "And poisoning is such a highly specialized industry nowadays!"

"Then the world says: Individualism or Socialism? I know myself that our present industrial system is enough to make a cat laugh, and an angel weep. But I read a book—I am always reading books—which tells me that, if we have public ownership, my individuality will be kneaded into an amorphic mass . . . . or mess, I forget which. I don't want to be kneaded into either. Going home I am kept waiting five, ten, thirty minutes for my train. Like any other gentleman I mutter: Bless these railway directors! Some red-tie overhears me. He insists on linking me into my compartment, and assaults me with Socialist principles and Prussian statistics until my head reels, and my individualism with it."

"You have at least the comfort that goes with an open mind?"

"An open mind brings about as much comfort as an open door on a sleety day in January. Militarism or Pacifism? I dislike killing: that makes me the one. I dislike the German syntax: that makes me the other. Free Trade or Tariff Reform I have happily been able to postpone."

"Indeed!" I said.

"Yes," he iterated firmly. "There is such a jolly scuffle going on between the various tariffs in their own kennel that I can wait till the winning dog emerges. But then: Bacon or Shakespeare? John Masefield or . . . . poetry? And so on, for the path between these antitheses leads to the world's end and dips over into infinity."

After a pause, he went on:

"Have the courtesy at least not to mention Hamlet, a detestable play in which the supreme intellectual

problem, that of evidence, is solved in terms of Drury
Lane. . . . I have not spoken of such minor but
besetting dubieties as: When shall we have a General
Election? Who will win the Cricket Championship?"

"Still," I said, "If we are to live at all we must
have a point of view, a philosophy."

"Philosophy," he replied, "is a blanket which men
have woven to protect themselves against life, which
is, I suggest, on the whole something of a frost.
When more than usually frightened they pull the
blanket up over their heads. But I too have mine.
Did you ever see a weather-vane?"

"Really," I was beginning.

"Most people know it only as a literary image.
A weather-vane is a very insubstantial, rotatory
object set on a very substantial, fixed object, say, a
tin arrow on a cathedral. My public self is the tin
arrow which whirls round with every breeze. My
reserve personality is the cathedral. That it is there
I know: what it is like I can in no way discover. I
follow the most popular of all religions, the religion
of never giving yourself away."

Then, catching at an unspoken question:

"How I earn my living? I don't. I am a gentleman of independent means. This religion of mine
is fully furnished. It, too, if we may continue the
figure, has its cathedral: that vastest and most
splendid of all contemporary buildings, the hotel.
It has its seven sacraments: the cheque-book, the
motor-car, the golf-links, the chef, and . . . . why
yes! . . . . three whiskey-and-sodas. Good night!"

The chair crunched departure. The Man who
has lost his Table of Values disappeared, and left
me staring into the darkness and the fires of night.

Our modern disease is not that we are proud, but
that we are proud about the wrong things. We
have gained the whole world, and cravenly cancelled
our own souls. Many of our popular novelists and
their readers are in the case of the king in the fairy-

tale : they are naked to all the winds. Human life needs a garment of philosophy if it is to endure, and they have none. If a man will but consent to accept that which has been woven for him by the secular labour of civilization out of many inter-mixed fibres —God, immortality, the Christian creed, marriage, property, and freedom—he need not shiver. As a magnet pulls into patterned order what was an incoherent mass of iron filings, so these central ideas send out a current of principle through the vast and amazing medley of modern life and literature.

It is because Mr. Chesterton and Mr. Belloc stand for these romantic and redeeming commonplaces that they are the greatest spiritual forces in English letters. But even they shine with a dimmed lustre. I cannot forgive Mr. Belloc that knock-about anarchism, which he mistakes for political health. And who can forgive Mr. Chesterton his awful jolliness? Show him a corpse, just fished out of the Thames, or the murderer of it, or an international financier, or any other hideous object, and he is off at once to dictate an article for the *Daily News*, explaining how awfully jolly the whole thing is. Optimism must dominate the orchestra, no doubt, but it ought to be played on discreetly muted strings.

We touch the highest wisdom when we learn to rejoice in our limitations. Why be angry at the narrowness of our compass, seeing that we have all eternity in which progressively to widen it? It braces the curious mind—and what is mind but curiosity?—to realize that, because of the inexhaustibility of knowledge, we are saved from all menace of tedium; that a new adventure awaits us behind every blade of grass; and that, released at last from the fetters of time and space, but not from those of individuality, our finitude will have scope to follow the old trail of infinity in an endless asymptote. Truly, narrow-mindedness is the beginning of wisdom.

NOVEMBER FIRST : THE DAY
OF ALL THE DEAD

Verlaine, to whom the whole rebellion of art
came under the form of music, in that mode also
experienced autumn. Not through the eye, as with
Keats, but through the ear her ambiguous beauty of
achievement and decay entered his soul. He heard
it as a long-sobbing violin, to which a tumult of
leaves and illusions, severed from the roots of life,
circled about in a grave saraband of despair. And
since music is, as it is, a food as fit for melancholy
as for love, the high road of initiation into death,
and the cradle-language of immortality, the exquisite
dereliction of the French poet does in truth evoke
the very spirit of this withering and sombre time.

Circumambient blue walls of mist close up our
horizons of hope, rising as Merlin's prison rises in
the saga. We feel a chill drowsiness flowing
through all the veins of existence : it is as if the
world, like Socrates, were dying from the feet up.
A wintry silence has fallen on the birds, if it be not
for that epitome of loneliness, the cry of the lapwing,
or the clangour of rooks or of wedged battalions of
wild geese, cleaving the emptiness of the sky.

Over all this ritual of desolation the trees prevail,
towering above the rout like the captains of a
defeated army. The flame of October has burned
itself out ; the glory of red and orange, and bronze
which wrapped the woods in a conflagration of
beauty has smouldered down to faint embers. The
oak still keeps its leaf, and here and there the eye
encounters the bulk of an elm, not yet denuded, or

the lyrical gleam of a birch that has so far missed
its cue of departure. But as for the rest, they are
no more than a shuddering nakedness. To Verlaine,
as to all the poets, they are the wailing violins or
lutes of the storm. Along many an avenue or
canal as gracious as that which Hobbima painted,
the poplars stand up above the dim water like
candlesticks of mourning set beside a catafalque.
In truth they are the funeral torches of autumn.

The poets, since poetry first was, have recorded
all this spectacle of decadence with the faithful
agony with which one records the oncoming of death
over the lineaments of a beloved face. In magic of
description there is hardly anywhere a touch that
excels the "leopard woods" and "mouse-coloured
waters" celebrated by Mr. Yeats. As for symbol-
ism and philosophy, all the singers are but too prone
to sentimentalize themselves into a mere pagan
cowardice of despair. Religion alone confronts
material dissolution with right courage—the courage
of the faith that looks through death.

For it is no chance, but a deliberate choice, that
consecrates this grey prologue of winter to the
memory of "All the Dead." Not a village in France
—the true Catholic France—but will see to-day the
last flowers of the year strewn, for a festival in which
belief almost becomes vision, over graves at which
the elders will kneel, and the children be not forbidden to play. In Tyrolese hamlets the little fonts
of holy water that hang by every tombstone, however wretched, will be filled for sprinkling, and
the bells rung.

In many an Irish farmhouse or cottage, where
the old customs are not wholly forgotten, the hearth
will be clean swept, and a new fire laid down, with
a chair set before it for every member of the household who has passed *ex umbris et imaginibus*. For
it is thought that they are privileged to revisit to-

night the place of their childhood. Dead names
will be cried about the winds, the names of those
who achieved, the names of those who were broken
or who broke themselves. Not a heart but about
its portals there will flutter a strange drift of memories, for it is the Day of All the Dead. Happy—
thrice happy in " drear-nighted November "—is the
faith of those for whom the dead have gone not into
the night, but into the light.

THE IMPORTANCE OF BEING NARROW-MINDED

The attempt of any individual mind to come to terms with the modern world as a whole is like an attempt to decant the Atlantic into a thimble.

Every contemporary book is a record of the fashion in which some particular thimble was defeated, and of the mood or the philosophy in which it accepted its defeat. The characteristic note of our day is not pride. It is not Professor Schäfer's threat that, if we are not very nice to him, he will one day manufacture a frog out of an old pair of boots and a bowl of sugar. Nor is it the graver threat of the Eugenic Society that, if we are very nice, they will arrange for the birth of a race of beings so glorious as to be indistinguishable from the members of their own committee. Nor that less scientific and more tolerable will-o'-the-wisp, the Superman, lately deceased; nor any other proclamation of our imminent omnipotence.

On the contrary, it is the re-discovery of the intoxicating fact that man is finite, fallible, prone to sin, dyspepsia, and influenza, and that, in general, he is rather small beer. Lord Rosebery, for instance, is so annoyed at an inspection of the shelves laden with books which he cannot possibly read, that he invites us to put a match to every library, and cremate those corpses which poison his originality. Mr. Balfour retires from public leadership, explaining that politics have become so complicated that he is unable to understand them any longer, and must delegate that task to Mr. Bonar Law. Not inappropriately he writes an article on M. Bergson, that philosopher of the tea-table, who has discarded the understanding altogether in favour of the much more agreeable faculty of intuition.

Mr. H. G. Wells, having set the hero of his last novel, "Marriage," thinking about modern life through several hundred monologues, unloaded on a very patient young lady, is obliged to send both of them to Labrador to cool their heads. It is rumoured that Mr. Shaw is about to write to the *Times*, explaining that he once—although, of course, only once—made a mistake. As for Mr. Belloc and Mr. Chesterton, they may be counted on to continue wallowing in their respective humilities till the end of time, and probably well on into eternity.

Of the proved inadequacy of the thimble there can, therefore, be no doubt. In the face of it, two attitudes are possible. The first is that of the boy who, in presence of the Christmas pudding, is plunged into the sourest pessimism by the discord which manifests itself in him between desire and capacity. The other is that of M. Renan, who, on leaving the great Paris Exhibition in which, in glittering avenue after avenue, the glory of civilization had filled his eyes, exclaimed: "*Mon Dieu*! How many exquisite things there are which one can do without!" Our choice lies between the distended depression of the schoolboy and the smiling asceticism of M. Renan: the former is, I fear, more typical of our time.

Indeed, most of our contemporaries are infinitely angry at not being infinite. So much happiness, so much exultant life, and they are allowed to drink only some of it—not all! Such a bewildering multiplicity of books, of people, and they are suffered to dip a mere liqueur glass out of the ocean! When Professor Schäfer does produce his frog, these gourmands of experience will envy the unhappy animal his froggishness—a whole area of sensation from which they are shut out. This crowded complexity of life has touched many of our finest minds. It tortures Mr. Wells with a metaphysical headache. It so affects Mr. Arnold Bennett that in his recent novels, if the hero meets a policeman and a porter at a railway station, you may safely expect a footnote or an inset advertisement announcing that in 1914 Mr. Bennett will publish, in a further supplementary novel, the spiritual history of the policeman, and in 1916 that of the porter.

The late Professor William James, in his Ingersol lecture on immortality, finds it facing him in an even grimmer form. Since everybody is immortal, and since, on his cheerful hypothesis, everybody is going to Heaven, we are confronted with a horrible prospect of Paradisaical congestion. But he considerately goes on to observe that, on the other side of the grave, each of us will continue to exist only as a point of view, and that you can fit any number of points of view into a given space, and still more into that which confesses no bondage at all to space.

Great consolation for those whose only trouble about human life is that there is so much of it, is to be found in three central truths which, for the sake of simplicity, we may call the I-ness of the I, the *hic et nunc*-ity of consciousness, and the *ad hoc*-ness of action. Expressed in the obscurer language of everyday, this means that you are yourself, mainly because you are nobody else, and that your particular mind exists in a particular body at a particular time in a particular place, with its energies mortgaged to particular pursuits, chiefly that of getting enough to eat. And, so far from these gyves hampering, they actually enfranchise you. They may shut you out from the Riviera, but they admit you to the empyrean. Your study window, however small, is large enough to contain the whole procession of the stars, and if you dig deep enough in your back garden, you will come on the flaming genesis of the world.

202

THE UNIMPORTANCE OF POLITICS

This is no "withering denunciation" or "scathing exposure" of those ambassadors at the Court of Notoriety whom we style politicians. Nobody is "branded" in it as a traitor, an anarchist, an incendiary, an elderly King's Counsel, a cabbage-headed mule, an ill-masked Fenian, a certificated despatch-rider, a village ruffian, or even a disliker of legal blasphemy. It goes simply upon a large fact as to which there can be no dispute, and asks whether that fact is of good or of evil countenance. The fact in question is that we are all politicians now. Certain albino blotches do indeed run counter to type, prigs for the most part, but with that exception we are all tarred with the same brush. Is the brush too heavily charged, too industrious and wide-wandering? Do we assign disproportionate importance to *homo politicus*, with his equipment of masks and megaphones? Do we, in short, gesture and bellow too much for the good of our souls? It cannot be too clearly understood that the line of approach to the enquiry is not Olympian, but confessional. Any of us is ready enough to admit that there are too many of the other kind of fellow about. For me, the appearance of a thing called Unionism, for instance, is numbered among the darkest and least penetrable mysteries. On the other hand it has long since been suggested that the world would go much better if Ireland was towed into mid-Atlantic, and sunk. Some Radicals could spare a coronet or two without tears, or indeed the whole practice of coronetcy in general, while some Dukes are convinced that there is exactly one Lloyd-George in excess of requirements. Such conclusions are easy to reach, but they are vain. The only real problems are those that concern the inner life, and its institution in wisdom. And the suggestion of this paper is that we make overmuch of politics. We cheat ourselves. Our days are only twenty-four hours broad, and not more than sixty years long, truncated by sleep and sickness. We have, as we say, a terrible lot of things to get through, and if we give to any of them, and especially to the poorer sort, too much head-tumult and heart-break, we are betrayed and undone.

It is necessary to begin by repudiating that view which would dismiss politics as mere sham and rococo. Job himself might well lose patience, as indeed he did, with such chatter. The State does not argue, it imposes itself. The only sanctuary of escape from it is the lunatic asylum. It is the raw material in which we have all got to work, without which we can do nothing. The particular State to which any of us belongs is a moment of equilibrium, stable or unstable, in the secular scuffle for the ownership of the two most real things we know, land and men. So real is the fight for these ingredients of welfare that there is not the least prospect of its ever reaching a term. The porcupine image, employed by Schopenhauer, is rich in suggestion. Seeing men not as trees walking, but as porcupines grubbing, he points out that the task of society is to bring its units so close together that they shall keep one another warm, and to keep them as far apart as will secure each against the bristling quills of his neighbours. The process of re-arrangement goes on without break or respite. Who is to stand where? Each porcine group has its own notion, accompanied by a map with a statistical appendix;

no two maps agree, and there is a continual stir of hustling and shouldering in the mass. And, for all their trouble, colds and blood-letting are more frequent than the ideal disposition. If you are very dainty, you may call the affair rather disreputable, and decidedly mixed. Nothing human is alien from that fate. But to call it unreal would be a sad absurdity. Moreover, its scope is as wide as civilization. No provision has been made for disinterested spectators. The Lucretian tower of ivory was found, when completed, to be too frail for habitation, and the judgment-seat of Gallio was long since broken up for firewood.

The first note of politics, then, is not unreality and remoteness, but on the contrary, intimate and dominant reality. The second is, beyond all doubt, unreason. The late William James records the inspiration of one of those founders of minor religions, the names of which sound like a disease : this prophet felt that " he had fire enough in his belly to burn up all the sins of the world." That is the sort of thing that fashions the course of politics. Movements which are, in the last analysis, not exactly blind appetites, but at any rate Bergsonian waves of appetency, accomplish themselves, if they have vitality enough, if not, they simply break in foam, and disappear. In neither case has reason, mere platform and newspaper reason, created the event out of its entrails. Ireland—if I may again use her as an illustration—has not argued or even fought, she has simply lived her way back to some sort of autonomy. I must not be understood as denying that there is in politics such a phenomenon as conversion. But it is much more commonly catastrophic than discursive. The mind is not a scientific balance, delicately responsive to the differential ounce : it is much more like a home-made bomb which quite dramatically explodes. In

England what usually happens is that an elector sees suddenly that something or other is a damned shame, and decides to vote the other way next time. The moving consideration may be, and often is, trivial, irrelevant, or dead : an enquirer, reading Irish history for the first time, for instance, becomes a Home Ruler in order to let Queen Elizabeth and Oliver Cromwell know what he thinks of their disgusting conduct. But such illumination very seldom results from a course of Hansard, or systematic attendance at meetings of the opponent colour. Your typical party leader does not even aim at convincing his enemies, he makes speeches in order to explain himself to his friends. And your sound party man is a good deal more of the mystic than of the rationalist. Loyalty, to him, consists in accepting not the known thing which his leader said yesterday, but the unknown thing which he will say to-morrow. The disbelief in the arbitrament of reason, which lurks under so many forms of controversy, finds by times an even franker expression. The gospel of violence was never preached from such high places, or with so confident a challenge, as in this mellow age of sociology. Arson has become the paltriest of incidental by-play. The right of rebellion at haphazard, as one may say, has received ceremonial sanction at the very fountain-head of law.

These facts may please or displease us, but at any rate they are facts. And, whether pleased or not, a prudent man will adjust himself to facts. What is the general scheme of our adjustment ? Mainly noise. We have with loving care created an apparatus of clamour from which none can escape, to which none can listen without the gravest disturbance of judgment. We all shout so loudly that nobody hears his own voice. We wallow in a sea of leading articles. We cram ourselves into drab and draughty halls, we slap our knees in railway-carriages, we rattle the plates at dinner with dialectic vehemence, we sleep on the preparation of nasty epigrams, we muddy our souls with that form of art known as the "thumping poster." It is necessary for our comfort that our opponents should be daily convicted, not only of scoundrelism wholesale, but of scoundrelism retail. Every day must furnish a new crisis, and an unprecedented betrayal. No Shop Hours Act shall procure them a half-day's respite ; the peace of Sunday itself would be intolerable if it were not punctuated with thunder. It would be no fantastic definition of an "active politician " to say that he is a man who is always arguing with another man, without ever seeing the other man's point. Now it may be urged that this way of going-on proves at least that we take politics seriously, and treat it with respect due to it as the most important of secular realities. But in fact it proves the contrary. The true human response to real things is not garrulity, but action. People who talk daggers incessantly do not, as a rule, use even bodkins. And if the excessive word is, in general, at enmity with the necessary deed, there are features even more disabling in the special case with which we are occupied. It is the old story of destroying emphasis by emphasizing everything. We have all met the student who does not feel at home with his text-book until he has underlined every sentence in it. Political controversy—one had better say gladiator-dom—is deeply infected with the same illusion. All the little fishes in it talk like whales. The youngest of us has lived through such a succession of "tremendous crises " and "turning points in the march of progress," he has seen the "final ruin of the Empire " accomplished, "civilization outraged " and "purity of administration poisoned at its very source" so often, and on the other hand, has participated in so many of the "greatest steps forward in our time and generation" that he has become, or ought to have become, somewhat critical and even callous. The schoolboy who had been to *Julius Cæsar* expressed himself as jolly glad that he had not been born in ancient Rome: it was blank verse all the time, and he was sure that he never could have managed it. It is just as severe a tax on the ordinary mind to live in a political world in which it is Armageddon or the New Jerusalem all the time.

If garrulity, then, weakens the faculty and debauches the aim of action, can it be justified on the ground that it makes converts? Even if this plea be stated at its strongest it will not, I think, be found adequate: the size of the crop is no return for the seed scattered, and the cost of the sowing. The process of conversion is, as has been suggested, freaky, erratic, and not reducible to any clear principles of causation. The man who is led to change sides by a little silent, stiff reading of books must not be credited as a gain to the diurnal apparatus of controversy with which we are now dealing. That forbids silence, and does not express itself in the spacious solidity of books. Indeed, English literature, so rich in everything else, is singularly poor in what may be called books of induction into politics. Other turnovers are referable to other motives. An elector will discover, for instance, that the leaders of his party have expunged the *not* from a commandment which had previously been held fundamental. He does not leave the party, the party leaves him. The entrance of others into the new light is consequent upon careful study, and a sound prognostic, of the phenomenon of feline saltation. These are not, in the strict sense, converts; this point of view is indeed often pressed upon them with a certain harshness of language. But it ought to be noted in their favour that they are among the most trustworthy of politicians. You always know where to find them;

you have only to go to the winning side. Further defections and adhesions are to be ascribed to family affection. A nephew, or a son-in-law, or the son of a friend, is seeking a public career in the opposite camp, and an elector, previously Blue, will vote Yellow in order to give the young fellow a leg up. The damned-shame theory will be found to cover most of the remainder, and this involves a mystical passion which is not really explicable at all in terms of the platform. We must not, of course, ignore the cardinal consideration that most people are not convertible at all, and are never converted. Things go against them, it is true, and they are left bewailing the wholesomer past, and fighting a hopelesss rear-guard action against the triumphant evil of the present. Their children growing up in the shadow of the accomplished fact do not have to renounce the prejudices of their fathers : they are simply born on the other side, and there is an end of the matter. Whether a psychology of these processes can be constructed is doubtful : certainly they root deeply in human nature. Every habit is a sort of organic Toryism, every idea is a Radical, at least *in potentia*. We cannot very well get on without some equipment of both, and the harmony established between them, early or late, determines our politics. It is not established without a struggle. It is not only in Tartaran of Tarascon that two personalities conflict, the one calling to labour and glory, the other to old slippers and familiar delights. Some balance we must reach between what is and what might be, and most of us reach it pretty soon. We attach ourselves to some *ism*, and spend the rest of our lives in discovering gradually what it means, and why we believe it to be right. We certainly do not need, morning and evening, tonic draughts of dialectic to confirm us. They do not make our faith better, and

they do keep us in a fret of censoriousness, a ferment
of self-praise, which cannot be good for anybody.

Our hygiene of intellect is then demonstrably at
fault, very much at fault. The endless iteration to
which we decree ourselves is defended as a necessary
means of "keeping the party's pecker up." M.
Sorel would, perhaps, think it more dignified to
speak of the perpetuation of the myth, or poetical
lie, which, in his interpretation, inspires each group
to the conquest of truth. Some eager spirits cannot
be happy unless they are constantly "rubbing it in,"
as if wisdom was a sort of embrocation, and others
conceive their art as a form of hypnotism. This last
is the central aud common idea, and the slightest
examination of it condemns our procedure. Our
methods produce boredom, and boredom happens to
be the one condition of mind that makes hypnotism
impossible. No one can be hypnotised without
intense concentration on his part, generated by
acute interest. And if our conduct of the intellect
is foolish, the attitude of our wills is almost wicked.
We ascribe to certain lines of policy—our own
programme, to wit—a magic potency and fruitfulness
which we well know they do not possess. We
deceive the young with extravagant hopes, the failure
of which plunges them into that calf-melancholy
which they call "disillusionment." We mislead the
poor with promises grossly in excess of the limitations
of political reform. This is no special vice of any
particular party; we are all in the same boat. There
is involved, be it noted, a grave offence to human
nature. We reduce the integral man to the status
of a mere political unit, and we then reduce his
politics to terms of a single factor. We treat him,
not as a man, but as an aspect of a point of view.
The fiscal controversy furnishes a clinching example
of this. We know that external trade policy is only
one element in the complicated web of causation

that makes nations prosperous or miserable. We know that, whatever else may be said about the sort of Protection proposed, the one thing certain is that a scheme so limited will not make much difference one way or the other. But we talk on both sides as if nothing else in the world counted, or mattered. Our pockets bulge with quack Utopias for sale to the crowd: "Free Trade and big loaves for everybody," "Tariff Reform and fine jobs for everybody." We even insult other nations with our rhetoric. Germany, the United States, France, are all Hells on earth or Heavens on earth according to our bias: none of them is allowed to be merely an earth on earth. This habit of over-crying our goods is so deeply enregistered in us that any lapse attracts attention. Our Irish realism, for instance, is over-whelmed with reproaches. English observers are shocked or, as the case may be, exultant at what they call our lack of enthusiasm at the approach of Home Rule. They expect rhapsodies and sunbursts, and are bewildered to find only very earnest discussions of the probable influence of autonomy on taxation and tweed, on bad roads and the beef export. Every sin against the set limits of life, every breaking of bounds by the practical imagination, carries its own retribution with it. In the present instance the penalty is heavy. It consists in the ruling out of politics of the experimental method, and this is a great misfortune. For the normal man is not, of his own choice, a prophet. Faced with one of those vast and serious problems of our intricate modern life, his own impulse would lead him to try some solution, to see how it worked, and to learn from experience. Such scientific modesty is not permitted us. The politician who does not dogmatize in advance of the facts is lost. Success is to the man who is more cocksure about everything than anybody ought to be about anything. The Myth exacts its sacrifices.

Is there to be discerned any promise of relief? It may, I think, be said that there is a glimmer, faint but perceptible. The first condition of a cure is certainly present, namely, a realization of the fact of disease. There is a general, vague sense of malaise, a feeling that the place of politics in the communal life is not what it was, and that new adjustments are necessary. The suggestion appears in many shapes, some of them extremely questionable. The protest, or rather, the riot in ink associated with the names of Mr. Belloc and the Messrs. Chesterton, is perhaps the most respectable, although it is by no means tiresomely respectable. Men of true literary genius are nearly always feverish and incompetent politicians, and these men of genius have not escaped the laws of their temperament. No movement was ever before so brilliantly, and so variously wrong. Their campaign is wrong in principle, in aim, in method, and in temper. I doubt whether their followers understand in any sort of vital way the full menace and horror of their programme. Roughly it amounts to an assertion that the ordinary citizen is insufficiently interested in the conduct of the State. At present he spends only about half his spare time talking politics; in future he must so spend it all. He must follow, clause by clause, the business of Parliament, instant to detect tyranny in a comma, and enslavement in a schedule. The party system—that convenient canalization of political effort—must disappear. Every voter must be his own leader: he must whip himself up every day to whatever scratch dominates his conscience for the time being. As for his general attitude towards Parliament and the members of it, instruction in detail cannot be given, but it must be one of contempt. Only thus can the people enter into its heritage. Such a programme affects me like something half way between a pantomime and a nightmare. It stupefies, it overwhelms. And why has it been formulated? Because Mr. Belloc discovered that Ministers sometimes promote their relatives, and Mr. Chesterton discovered that they sometimes dip their pannikins into the milky flood of the Stock Exchange. To strike upon a motive so trivial was bad enough; still worse is it that the blow should have come from Brutus. One could understand a machine-shop Socialist like Mr. Wells, whose very dreams must glisten like polished steel, kicking his world to pieces because a few specks of dust have got into the mechanism. But Mr. Belloc and Mr. Chesterton cannot do so without a complete abandonment of their philosophy. The very spiritual essence of them was that they spoke up for the warm, fallible, and human man against the bloodless-perfect phantasms and categories. And now they suddenly denounce walking because you cannot walk without compromising the unsullied cleanness of your boots. Losing a ship for the lack of a ha'porth of tar was nothing to this: they desert the ship because a few drops of tar have been spilled on her snowy deck. Coventry Patmore says somewhere that belief in man's perfectability on earth is the last proof of insanity. That is sound Catholic doctrine, full of good sense and intelligent humility. Nobody knows better than the authors of the League for Clean Government that there never existed, and never will exist, in this world an absolutely clean government. There runs through the whole of the material a certain obvious flaw which inhibits any such ideal sculptor—that flaw which is known to the highest science as Original Sin. The devil is not dead, and he does not neglect his business. Wherever you look, whether in the State or in the human organization of the Church, you are bound to find a leaven of corruption. To suggest that in our time, and not before it, this leaven has become more noticeable and more dangerous is a flat denial of facts of which neither Mr. Belloc nor the Messrs. Chesterton would be guilty. One must reluctantly charge them with the gravest of all political offences : they have disturbed the soul of youth with impossible dreams. They have committed high treason against the decent finitude of life. To the workers, rejoicing in their newly-won safeguard against destitution, they have cried out a learned jeer about bread and circuses : by telling men authoritatively that they were slaves they have in truth enslaved them. These are sad divagations, and they point to a future even more sinister. Let Mr. Gilbert Chesterton keep company for even a little longer with these inhuman cleannesses, and he will end up as President of the Eugenic Society. His brother will likely become not merely a Dickensian, but a real barrister. Mr. Belloc, who is an excellent economist, will wake up to find himself promoting a company to suppress company promoting.

The truth is that the party machine is necessary, and that it is very far from being a necessary evil. Only by acceptance, and the right use of it, can the ordinary citizen hope to live at his maximum of political efficiency, and at the same time keep something of himself for that more secret spiritual activity which, for lack of a better name, is called culture. If political life is to continue at all, bodies of men must agree to act together. The moment they decide on such general action—naturally on the basis of ideas held in common—a party organization creates itself. A constitution, officers, committees, inner committees spring almost spontaneously into existence. The subscriptions that needs must be levied generate that awful fact, a party fund. What is there to quarrel with ? For any individual member of such a body to complain that he cannot express through it his whole mind and temperament is absurd: it is like condemning a garden spade because you cannot shave with it. There is no foreshortening, and no oppression of conscience. Matters on which we differ are left outside, as not relevant to our limited and special purpose. And party programmes are not static formulæ, but organic growths. If it seems to us that ours ought to develop in certain directions it is our task to explain, to argue, to canvass, to force our new ideas into it by the pressure of vitality. Contempt for the technical forms, under which laws are both made and administered, is a wholesome exuberance of the young. It helps to preserve the spirit from the letter that kills, but it does not affect the clear necessity for some sort of letter. Ritual is of the essence of social organization. An anarchist may deny all authority, but you cannot have a meeting of anarchists without a chairman set in authority over it. Contempt for politicians, for the type of personality produced by their calling, is a still poorer foundation. It is significant that the only skilled pursuit in which the amateur sneers at the professional is politics. The sneer is, moreover, wholly unjustified. The ethical level of contemporary "professional" politics is certainly higher than that of contemporary business; its intellectual level is certainly higher than that of contemporary literature. And, of the three, the public man has the hardest task set him. He is the only citizen who is obliged to choose omniscience for his specialism. The nature of the relationship binding him to his constituents is one of the most baffling cases in casuistry, and it is for him an acute and daily problem. No other man is asked to drive so difficult a pair of chariot-horses as his of private ambition and public duty. We must not idealize, but to me he seems to make rather a better hand of his exacting trade than we make of ours. It is the fashion to speak of the qualities requisite for political life as altogether paltry and undistinguished. M. Clémenceau, for instance, when asked the other day what were the claims of M. Doumergue to the Premiership, replied : " He has a very loud voice." But aptitude, ranging from average talent to decisive genius, is a force just as dominant and unmistakable in the profession of politics as in any other. The contention that the pecuniary rewards are extravagant cannot be treated seriously. You can have two Members of Parliament at the nominal cost of one middling Civil Servant, and at a much lower real cost. A greed that is satisfied with £400 a year is much too modest to be dangerous.

The politician invites ridicule when with Mr. Lloyd George he calls himself the priest of humanity. If his fun`tion sometimes approaches the sacerdotal, it bears, at other times, a strong resemblance to that of the scavenger. It is a specialized calling, made necessary by our complex civilization, no better and no worse than any other. You become master of the masters of it not by barren abuse, but by fruitful acceptance. In my native city it used to be a bye-word of folly that a man should hire a cab and run after it. There is no better wisdom in creating a highly articulated system of delegation, conference, and enactment, and then proceeding to do personally the work that we have deputized. That citizen economizes his energy best, who concerns himself only with large principles, and leaves to his appropriate specialist all matters of technique. There is involved no peril to freedom. The "insolence of elected persons " which angered Walt Whitman is not in truth formidable. Go beyond their time they cannot, and, if they go beyond their programme, the evil can only be temporary. The community at large is amply protected, protected above all by that very palladium of liberty, the Right to Yawn.

UNIMPORTANCE OF POLITICS

Freezing, which is merely the yawn of water, will crumble any rock. Gulliver, in the fable, delivers himself from the mesh woven about his sleep by the Liliputians by the simple process of stretching himself. The national organism best repels outrage not by incessant twitchings, but by long, receptive, silent accumulations of force duly discharging themselves in the end in that muscular avalanche of a yawn which is styled a General Election. In addition to this regimen there is, of course, need also of a philosophy. One does not like to use the term pessimism; it is a word that has kept very queer company in its day. If you so much as suggest that you cannot make a silk purse out of a sow's lugs, make a pint pot hold a quart, or butter parsnips with soft words, the odds are that somebody will call you a pessimist, or even a dyspeptic crank. But it is very advisable that, at a reasonably raw age, a citizen should, like Arnold, or rather Empedocles, decide to nurse no extravagant hope. Politics can never be the architect of the New Jerusalem: it is not cut out to be much more than a speculative, suburban builder. It is, as Lord Morley says, eminently the province of the second best. You cannot do anything in it without doing some harm. It is far from being a patent specific against all the ills that human hearts endure. Used in the way suggested it will give us a world just good enough to live in. So using it the citizen may hope to approximate to a frugal content. With hardly a pang of envy he will leave the Olympus of the illustrated papers to be ruled by Tango actresses, Cabinet ministers, authors, and the more select aud imaginative criminals. For his part he will ripen in the joyous humiliations of marriage, and the dynamic wisdom of the nursery. He will devote himself to those pursuits by which the soul of man is bettered: a reduction of his golf handicap, music, religion, and ascetical control of the enlarging girth. He will have time for picture-theatres, revues, aviation meetings, dinners to distinguished French Pagans, Sir George Alexander, Mr. Granville Barker, the Abbey Players, and Miss Horniman's repertory company. For crown of his happiness, he will also have time to read the admirable books of Mr. Belloc, and the two Chestertons, major and minor. He may even manage, although this is improbable, to keep within say two novels' length of Mr. Eden Philpotts, and three of Mr. Arnold Bennett, and to miss no more than four or five masterpieces of Mr. John Masefield in a lucky year. Upon this golden possibility I beg humbly to conclude.